# The Giant Book of Informative Facts

by
Jake Jacobs

* * * * *

Published by Jake Jacobs

The Giant Book of Informative Facts
Copyright© 2023 by Jake Jacobs

# 1.

Warner Bros. is one of the oldest and most prominent film studios in the world, founded on April 4, 1923, by brothers Harry, Albert, Sam, and Jack Warner.

# 2.

The studio was initially called "Warner Brothers Pictures, Inc." but later changed its name to Warner Bros. Pictures.

# 3.

The first film released by Warner Bros. was a silent film called "The Toll of the Sea" in 1922, which was notable for being one of the earliest color films.

# 4.

Warner Bros. gained significant success and recognition in the 1930s with the release of the groundbreaking film "The Jazz Singer" in 1927, which was the first feature-length film with synchronized sound.

# 5.

The success of "The Jazz Singer" propelled Warner Bros. into the era of "talkies" and cemented their reputation as innovators in the film industry.

# 6.

Warner Bros. has produced many iconic films over the years, including "Casablanca," "Gone with the Wind," "The Wizard of Oz," "The Shining," "Harry Potter," "The Dark Knight Trilogy," and "The Matrix."

# 7.

In 1948, Warner Bros. introduced the widescreen format with the release of "The Big Trail," pioneering a new era of cinematic presentation.

## 8.

Warner Bros. has been associated with several memorable characters and franchises, including Batman, Superman, Wonder Woman, Bugs Bunny, Daffy Duck, and Harry Potter.

## 9.

The Warner Bros. logo, featuring the Warner Bros. shield, has become an iconic symbol in the entertainment industry.

## 10.

Warner Bros. has diversified its operations beyond film production and distribution and has expanded into television production, music, video games, and theme parks.

## 11.

In 1955, Warner Bros. launched its television division, which has since produced numerous successful shows, such as "Friends," "The Big Bang Theory," "ER," and "The West Wing."

## 12.

Warner Bros. Records, established in 1958, has been home to many renowned musicians and bands, including Madonna, Prince, Neil Young, Fleetwood Mac, and Green Day.

## 13.

The acquisition of DC Comics in 1969 brought iconic superheroes like Batman and Superman under the Warner Bros. umbrella, leading to successful film franchises and merchandise.

## 14.

Warner Bros. Interactive Entertainment, the company's video game division, has published popular games such as the "Mortal Kombat" series, "Batman: Arkham" series, and "LEGO" video games.

## 15.

The Warner Bros. Studio Lot in Burbank, California, is a historic site and home to numerous sound stages, backlots, and iconic sets.

## 16.

The "Warner Bros. Water Tower," a recognizable landmark on the studio lot, has appeared in many Warner Bros. films and television shows.

## 17.

Warner Bros. has a strong presence in the global film industry, with international divisions and subsidiaries in countries like the United Kingdom, Japan, Germany, and Australia.

## 18.

Warner Bros. has received numerous accolades over the years, including Academy Awards, Golden Globe Awards, and Grammy Awards.

## 19.

Warner Bros. is known for its commitment to diversity and inclusion in the entertainment industry and has championed initiatives to promote underrepresented voices in film and television.

## 20.

In 1984, Warner Bros. became the first major Hollywood studio to establish a program to restore and preserve its classic films.

## 21.

The Warner Bros. Studio Tour, open to the public, offers visitors a behind-the-scenes look at the studio lot, showcasing iconic sets, props, costumes, and memorabilia.

## 22.

The Warner Bros. Animation division has produced popular animated TV shows, such as "Animaniacs," "Batman: The Animated Series," "Looney Tunes," and "Justice League Unlimited."

## 23.

Warner Bros. has a rich history of producing successful movie musicals, including "Singin' in the Rain," "The Music Man," "A Star is Born," and "Chicago."

## 24.

Warner Bros. has also ventured into the realm of live theater, producing successful stage adaptations of its films, such as "Elf: The Musical" and "Charlie and the Chocolate Factory."

## 25.

The Warner Bros. Studio Store, which was a chain of retail stores selling merchandise related to Warner Bros. films and characters, operated from 1991 to 2001.

## 26.

Warner Bros. has made significant contributions to the development of special effects and visual effects in the film industry, pioneering techniques that revolutionized movie-making.

## 27.

The Warner Bros. Studio Lot has served as the filming location for numerous iconic TV shows, including "Friends," "The Big Bang Theory," "Gilmore Girls," and "The West Wing."

## 28.

Warner Bros. has a long-standing partnership with director Christopher Nolan, resulting in critically acclaimed films such as "Inception," "The Dark Knight Trilogy," and "Dunkirk."

## 29.

The Warner Bros. Studio Lot has a rich history of hosting legendary directors, actors, and actresses, who have left their mark on the industry through their work on the lot.

## 30.

The "Warner Bros. Studio Museum" is currently being developed as an interactive museum experience to showcase the studio's history and contributions to the entertainment industry.

## 31.

Warner Bros. has produced successful animated feature films, including "The Iron Giant," "The LEGO Movie," "The LEGO Batman Movie," and "Happy Feet."

## 32.

The Warner Bros. Pictures logo has undergone several redesigns and variations over the years, evolving to reflect the changing trends and visual styles of the film industry.

## 33.

Warner Bros. has expanded its presence in the streaming market with the launch of the subscription-based streaming service, HBO Max, which offers a vast library of films and TV shows.

## 34.

Warner Bros. has been a pioneer in the adoption of digital technologies, embracing advancements in CGI, motion capture, and digital distribution to enhance the filmmaking process.

## 35.

The Warner Bros. Studio Lot has been a popular tourist attraction, drawing visitors from around the world who wish to experience the magic of the entertainment industry.

## 36.

The Warner Bros. Harry Potter Studio Tour in Leavesden, England, offers fans an immersive experience to explore the sets, props, and costumes used in the Harry Potter film series.

## 37.

Warner Bros. has a long-standing association with the Looney Tunes characters, such as Bugs Bunny, Daffy Duck, and Tweety Bird, which have become cultural icons.

## 38.

Warner Bros. has had successful partnerships with renowned directors, including Stanley Kubrick, Clint Eastwood, Martin Scorsese, and Tim Burton.

## 39.

The Warner Bros. Studio Lot has been used as a filming location for iconic films like "Casablanca," "The Matrix," "Blade Runner," "A Star is Born," and "Lethal Weapon."

## 40.

Warner Bros. has a significant presence in the global market, with distribution operations in over 125 countries.

## 41.

The Warner Bros. Studio Lot has been recognized as a historical landmark by the National Register of Historic Places, honoring its cultural and architectural significance.

## 42.

Warner Bros. has a strong commitment to philanthropy and has supported various charitable initiatives, including the "Warner Bros. Impact" program, which focuses on social responsibility.

## 43.

Warner Bros. has expanded its reach into the digital realm with the creation of interactive and mobile games based on its popular franchises, such as "Harry Potter: Wizards Unite."

## 44.

The WarnerBros. Consumer Products division licenses the Warner Bros. brand and characters for a wide range of merchandise, including toys, clothing, collectibles, and more.

## 45.

Warner Bros. has a rich history of producing successful television dramas, including "The Sopranos," "Game of Thrones," "The West Wing," and "Friends."

## 46.

Warner Bros. has collaborated with renowned filmmakers from around the world, fostering international co-productions and promoting diverse storytelling.

## 47.

The Warner Bros. Studio Lot has a state-of-the-art post-production facility, equipped with advanced technology for editing, sound mixing, and visual effects.

## 48.

Warner Bros. has embraced the digital era by venturing into online content distribution, launching platforms such as "DC Universe" for streaming DC Comics-related content.

## 49.

The Warner Bros. Studio Lot has served as a backdrop for various iconic car chase scenes in films like "Lethal Weapon," "Batman Begins," and "Mad Max: Fury Road."

## 50.

Warner Bros. has a dedicated animation division called Warner Bros. Animation, which has produced beloved animated TV shows and films like "Batman: The Animated Series," "Teen Titans Go!," and "The Lego Movie."

## 51.

Hulu was founded on October 29, 2007, as a joint venture between NBCUniversal, 21st Century Fox (now owned by The Walt Disney Company), and WarnerMedia (formerly Time Warner).

## 52.

The name "Hulu" is derived from a Mandarin Chinese term that means "gourd" or "calabash," symbolizing an empty vessel waiting to be filled with content.

## 53.

Hulu was initially created as a platform to stream television shows from major networks, offering users a way to watch their favorite shows online.

## 54.

The service launched to the public on March 12, 2008, with an ad-supported model that allowed users to watch select episodes of popular TV series.

## 55.

In 2010, Hulu launched a subscription-based service called Hulu Plus, which provided an expanded content library and access to full seasons of shows.

## 56.

Hulu Plus offered subscribers the ability to stream content on various devices, including computers, smartphones, tablets, gaming consoles, and smart TVs.

## 57.

In 2011, Hulu launched its first original series, "The Morning After," which was a daily recap show hosted by Brian Kimmet and Ginger Gonzaga.

## 58.

Hulu's first critically acclaimed original series was "The Handmaid's Tale," which premiered in 2017 and went on to win numerous awards, including Primetime Emmy Awards and Golden Globe Awards.

## 59.

Hulu has produced a wide range of original content across different genres, including dramas, comedies, documentaries, and animated series.

## 60.

Hulu has collaborated with prominent filmmakers and creators, such as J.J. Abrams, Mindy Kaling, Seth Rogen, and Jordan Peele, to produce original and exclusive content.

## 61.

In 2019, Disney acquired 21st Century Fox and gained majority control of Hulu, leading to a restructuring of ownership and strategy.

## 62.

With Disney's acquisition of Fox, Hulu became a part of Disney's streaming strategy alongside Disney+ and ESPN+.

# 63.

As of 2021, Hulu offers different subscription plans, including ad-supported and ad-free options, as well as bundles with Disney+ and ESPN+.

# 64.

Hulu has expanded its content library to include not only TV shows but also movies, documentaries, and original films.

# 65.

Hulu provides a platform for independent filmmakers and smaller studios to showcase their work through partnerships and distribution agreements.

# 66.

Hulu has partnered with various networks and studios to bring popular TV shows and movies to its platform, including ABC, NBC, Fox, FX, and the CW.

# 67.

In addition to current shows, Hulu has a large library of past seasons of popular series, making it a go-to destination for binge-watching.

# 68.

Hulu has also embraced the trend of live TV streaming, offering a Live TV service that allows subscribers to watch live broadcasts from major networks.

# 69.

Hulu offers a personalized recommendation system based on users' viewing history, helping them discover new shows and movies based on their preferences.

# 70.

In 2020, Hulu launched a user interface redesign, providing a more intuitive and streamlined experience for users across different devices.

## 71.

Hulu has become a key player in the streaming industry, competing with other major platforms like Netflix and Amazon Prime Video.

## 72.

Hulu has expanded its international presence through partnerships and licensing agreements with international networks and studios.

## 73.

Hulu has garnered critical acclaim for its original programming, with shows like "The Handmaid's Tale," "Ramy," and "PEN15" receiving praise from audiences and critics alike.

## 74.

Hulu has been recognized with numerous awards, including Primetime Emmy Awards, Golden Globe Awards, and Critics' Choice Television Awards.

## 75.

Hulu has developed a strong fan base for its original series, attracting dedicated audiences who eagerly anticipate new seasons and episodes.

## 76.

In 2021, Hulu launched Hulu + Live TV, a subscription plan that combines live TV streaming with on-demand content.

## 77.

Hulu has ventured into original documentaries, including "Fyre Fraud," "Hillary," and "Minding the Gap," showcasing a diverse range of non-fiction storytelling.

# 78.

Hulu has invested in international content, acquiring distribution rights to popular shows from other countries and bringing them to the U.S. audience.

# 79.

Hulu has experimented with innovative storytelling formats, including interactive shows like "You vs. Wild" and virtual reality (VR) experiences.

# 80.

The success of Hulu's original series has paved the way for increased investment in new and diverse voices in the entertainment industry.

# 81.

Hulu has become a platform for reboots and revivals of beloved TV shows, such as "Veronica Mars," "The X-Files," and "Animaniacs."

# 82.

Hulu has created a community and fan engagement through social media, where users can discuss and share their favorite shows and moments.

# 83.

The popularity of Hulu's original series has led to merchandise and spin-off opportunities, including books, clothing, and collectibles.

# 84.

Hulu has supported the LGBTQ+ community by producing and featuring shows that highlight LGBTQ+ stories and characters, such as "Love, Victor" and "Difficult People."

# 85.

Hulu has actively sought to amplify underrepresented voices in the industry, offering opportunities to diverse creators and talent.

# 86.

Hulu has collaborated with major sports leagues, such as the NBA, NFL, and NHL, to offer live sports programming to subscribers.

# 87.

Hulu has developed partnerships with other streaming services and platforms, including HBO Max, Starz, and Showtime, allowing users to access additional content through their Hulu subscription.

# 88.

Hulu has experimented with innovative advertising formats, including interactive ads and shorter ad breaks, providing a more engaging and personalized viewing experience.

# 89.

The success of Hulu's original content has led to international adaptations of its shows, allowing audiences worldwide to enjoy these stories.

# 90.

Hulu has provided opportunities for up-and-coming filmmakers and writers through its "Huluween" and "Hulu Originals Fellowship" programs.

# 91.

Hulu has supported various charitable initiatives, partnering with organizations like the Trevor Project and Red Nose Day to raise awareness and funds for important causes.

# 92.

The COVID-19 pandemic prompted Hulu to release certain films directly on its platform, allowing audiences to enjoy new releases from the comfort of their homes.

## 93.

Hulu has embraced diverse storytelling formats, including anthology series like "Castle Rock" and "Into the Dark," which feature standalone stories within a larger narrative framework.

## 94.

Hulu has launched exclusive international programming, including the critically acclaimed series "Normal People" and "The Great," expanding its reach beyond the United States.

## 95.

Hulu has been at the forefront of discussions around the future of streaming, adapting to evolving consumer preferences and technological advancements.

## 96.

The Hulu streaming platform is available on various devices such as smartphones, tablets, smart TVs, streaming devices, and gaming consoles, providing users with flexibility in accessing their favorite shows and movies.

## 97.

Hulu has fostered a collaborative relationship with its viewers, actively seeking feedback and suggestions to improve the user experience and content offerings.

## 98.

The success of Hulu's original content has attracted top-tier talent, with acclaimed actors, directors, and writers choosing to collaborate with the platform.

# 99.

Hulu has expanded its global presence through partnerships and licensing agreements, making its content available to viewers in different countries and regions.

# 100.

The evolution of Hulu from a platform primarily focused on streaming TV shows to a leading producer of original content has shaped the landscape of the streaming industry and contributed to the ongoing shift in how audiences consume entertainment.

# 101.

The Galapagos Great Blue Heron (Ardea herodias) is a species of heron found exclusively in the Galapagos Islands.

# 102.

It is one of the largest heron species in the Galapagos, with adults reaching up to 1.2 meters (4 feet) in height.

# 103.

The Great Blue Heron has a distinctive blue-gray plumage with a white head and a long, sharp beak.

# 104.

It is a solitary bird and is often found wading in shallow coastal waters or perched on rocks and branches near the water's edge.

# 105.

The Great Blue Heron is an opportunistic feeder and has a varied diet that includes fish, crustaceans, insects, and small mammals.

# 106.

It uses its long, sharp beak to spear its prey, making quick and precise strikes.

# 107.

The Galapagos Great Blue Heron is known for its patient hunting behavior, standing motionless for long periods of time before striking.

# 108.

It has excellent eyesight and can detect small movements in the water, allowing it to accurately target its prey.

# 109.

The Great Blue Heron is a skilled fisherman and is known to use various hunting techniques, including standing still, walking slowly, or even diving underwater to catch its prey.

# 110.

During breeding season, the Great Blue Heron displays elaborate courtship rituals, including aerial displays, bill clapping, and elaborate posturing.

# 111.

The heron builds its nest in trees or shrubs near the water's edge, using twigs and other vegetation to create a sturdy platform.

# 112.

The female typically lays 3-5 eggs, which both parents take turns incubating for around 27-30 days.

# 113.

The chicks hatch with a white downy plumage and are fed regurgitated food by their parents until they are able to catch their own prey.

# 114.

The Great Blue Heron has a lifespan of approximately 15 years in the wild.

## 115.

It is a non-migratory bird, meaning that it remains in the Galapagos Islands throughout the year.

## 116.

The Galapagos Great Blue Heron plays an important ecological role in the Galapagos ecosystem as a predator, helping to control the populations of its prey species.

## 117.

It is considered a flagship species for conservation efforts in the Galapagos Islands due to its unique habitat requirements and vulnerability to human disturbances.

## 118.

The Great Blue Heron is protected under the Galapagos National Park regulations, which prohibit disturbance or harm to the species.

## 119.

It is one of the iconic bird species that visitors to the Galapagos Islands often seek to observe and photograph.

## 120.

The Great Blue Heron has adapted to the harsh environmental conditions of the Galapagos, including strong winds, intense sun, and limited fresh water sources.

## 121.

It has long legs and toes, which are ideal for walking on uneven terrain and foraging in shallow waters.

# 122.

The Great Blue Heron has a complex vocal repertoire, including calls and squawks that are used for communication and territorial defense.

# 123.

It is known to engage in aggressive behaviors towards intruders, including wing-flapping, bill jabbing, and vocal displays.

# 124.

The Great Blue Heron has been observed using its wings to create shade while hunting, using the shadow to camouflage itself from its prey.

# 125.

It has a specialized neck vertebrae structure that allows it to strike with lightning-fast precision when catching prey.

# 126.

The Great Blue Heron has been known to steal food from other herons and birds, using its size and agility to intimidate and overpower competitors.

# 127.

The Galapagos Great Blue Heron is closely related to other heron species found around the world, including the American Great Blue Heron.

# 128.

The heron's presence in the Galapagos Islands is believed to be the result of a natural colonization event thousands of years ago.

# 129.

It is believed that the ancestors of the Galapagos Great Blue Heron arrived in the islands through natural dispersal or by hitching a ride on floating vegetation or debris.

## 130.

The Galapagos Islands provide a unique and isolated habitat for the Great Blue Heron, leading to the development of distinct characteristics and behaviors specific to this population.

## 131.

The Great Blue Heron is an indicator species, meaning that its presence and abundance can provide insights into the overall health and integrity of the Galapagos marine and coastal ecosystems.

## 132.

Climate change and rising sea levels pose a threat to the habitat of the Galapagos Great Blue Heron, as coastal areas and nesting sites may be impacted by increased erosion and flooding.

## 133.

Conservation efforts in the Galapagos Islands aim to protect the natural habitats of the Great Blue Heron and other native species, as well as to raise awareness about their ecological importance.

## 134.

Research and monitoring projects are ongoing to study the behavior, population dynamics, and breeding success of the Galapagos Great Blue Heron.

## 135.

The Galapagos Great Blue Heron is an important subject of scientific research, contributing to our understanding of avian ecology, evolution, and adaptation.

## 136.

The Galapagos Islands, including the habitat of the Great Blue Heron, are recognized as a UNESCO World Heritage Site due to their exceptional biodiversity and ecological significance.

## 137.

The Great Blue Heron's ability to thrive in the Galapagos Islands despite the challenges of limited resources and harsh conditions is a testament to its adaptability and resilience.

## 138.

The Galapagos Great Blue Heron is an important component of the Galapagos tourism industry, as visitors from around the world come to observe and appreciate its unique behaviors and natural beauty.

## 139.

Ecotourism activities in the Galapagos Islands adhere to strict guidelines to minimize disturbance to the Great Blue Heron and other wildlife, ensuring their long-term conservation.

## 140.

The Galapagos Great Blue Heron has become an iconic symbol of the Galapagos Islands and is featured in various promotional materials, including tourism brochures and documentaries.

## 141.

The heron's presence and abundance in the Galapagos ecosystem contribute to the overall ecological balance, as it plays a crucial role in controlling the populations of its prey species.

## 142.

The Galapagos Great Blue Heron is often observed in close proximity to marine iguanas, taking advantage of the iguanas' feeding activities to catch fish and other small marine organisms disturbed by their movement.

# 143.

The Great Blue Heron's feathers are adapted to repel water, helping it to stay dry and buoyant while foraging in wet environments.

# 144.

The heron's long legs and neck allow it to wade in deeper waters than most other bird species, giving it access to a wider range of prey.

# 145.

The Galapagos Great Blue Heron has a strong homing instinct, often returning to the same nesting site year after year.

# 146.

It has been observed using a variety of hunting techniques, including standing motionless, walking slowly, and performing quick lunges to catch prey.

# 147.

The heron's breeding season in the Galapagos Islands typically occurs from December to April, with males engaging in elaborate courtship displays to attract mates.

# 148.

The Great Blue Heron is highly adaptable, able to adjust its feeding and hunting strategies based on the availability of prey in its environment.

# 149.

The Galapagos Great Blue Heron is known to exhibit territorial behavior, defending its nesting sites and foraging areas from intruders.

# 150.

The conservation of the Galapagos Great Blue Heron and its unique habitat is a collective effort involving local communities, scientists, conservation organizations, and government agencies, aiming to ensure the long-term survival and protection of this remarkable species.

# 151.

The Galapagos Islands are home to four species of snakes: the Galapagos racer (Pseudalsophis biserialis), the Galapagos snake (Philodryas biserialis), the Galapagos giant snake (Chilabothrus angulifer), and the Galapagos banded snake (Clelia scytalina).

# 152.

The Galapagos racer is the most common and widespread snake species in the Galapagos Islands.

# 153.

The Galapagos racer is a non-venomous snake and feeds primarily on small vertebrates such as lava lizards and geckos.

# 154.

The Galapagos snake, also known as the banded snake or lava snake, is a non-venomous species that can reach lengths of up to 1.5 meters (5 feet).

# 155.

The Galapagos giant snake, also known as the Galapagos boa, is the largest snake species found in the Galapagos Islands, with individuals reaching lengths of up to 2.5 meters (8 feet).

# 156.

The Galapagos banded snake is a small snake species, usually measuring around 60 centimeters (2 feet) in length.

# 157.

Snakes are ectothermic animals, meaning they rely on external heat sources to regulate their body temperature.

## 158.

Due to their ectothermic nature, snakes in the Galapagos Islands are more active during warm periods and may hibernate or become less active during cooler seasons.

## 159.

Snakes play an important ecological role in the Galapagos Islands by helping to control populations of small vertebrates such as rodents and lizards.

## 160.

Snakes in the Galapagos Islands are generally not aggressive towards humans and will typically flee when encountered.

## 161.

The Galapagos Islands have a unique snake fauna, with the species having adapted to the isolated island environment over thousands of years.

## 162.

The limited presence of predators and competition has allowed Galapagos snakes to evolve into distinct species with specialized characteristics.

## 163.

Snakes in the Galapagos Islands have undergone unique evolutionary processes, resulting in variations in coloration and patterns compared to mainland snake species.

## 164.

The Galapagos racer is known for its slender body and dark coloration, which allows it to blend in with the volcanic rocks and vegetation of the islands.

## 165.

The Galapagos snake has a distinctive banded pattern, with alternating bands of dark and light coloration along its body.

## 166.

The Galapagos giant snake, also known as the Galapagos boa, has a robust body and can have various colorations, ranging from light brown to dark gray.

## 167.

The Galapagos banded snake has a pattern of thin dark bands along its body, which provides camouflage among the vegetation.

## 168.

Snakes in the Galapagos Islands are excellent climbers and are adapted to moving through rocky terrain and vegetation.

## 169.

The diet of Galapagos snakes primarily consists of small vertebrates, such as lava lizards, geckos, birds, and rodents.

## 170.

The snakes in the Galapagos Islands are capable of swallowing prey that is larger in diameter than their heads due to their highly flexible jaws.

## 171.

Snakes in the Galapagos Islands have adapted to the limited availability of freshwater by obtaining most of their water needs from their prey.

# 172.

The reproductive behavior of Galapagos snakes varies among species. Some species lay eggs, while others give birth to live young.

# 173.

Female Galapagos snakes typically produce a relatively small number of offspring per reproductive event, usually ranging from two to eight.

# 174.

Snakes in the Galapagos Islands play a vital role in nutrient cycling by consuming small vertebrates and releasing nutrients back into the ecosystem through their feces.

# 175.

The presence of snakes on the Galapagos Islands is an example of the adaptive radiation observed in the archipelago, where species have diversified to occupy specific ecological niches.

# 176.

The introduction of invasive species, such as rats and cats, has had a negative impact on native Galapagos snakes, as they prey on snake eggs and young individuals.

# 177.

Conservation efforts in the Galapagos Islands aim to protect the unique snake species and their habitats from threats such as habitat destruction and introduced predators.

# 178.

The Galapagos Islands are a UNESCO World Heritage Site and are protected by strict regulations to ensure the preservation of its unique flora and fauna, including snakes.

# 179.

Research and monitoring programs are conducted in the Galapagos Islands to better understand the ecology and behavior of native snake species.

# 180.

The Galapagos Islands offer unique opportunities for studying snake evolution and speciation due to their isolated nature and distinct environmental conditions.

# 181.

Galapagos snakes have been the subject of scientific studies examining their genetics, morphology, behavior, and ecological interactions.

# 182.

The adaptation and survival of snakes in the Galapagos Islands are closely linked to the availability of suitable habitat, including lava fields, rocky slopes, and vegetation-rich areas.

# 183.

Galapagos snakes exhibit behavioral adaptations to survive in the harsh island environment, such as thermoregulation to maintain body temperature and strategies for locating prey.

# 184.

The Galapagos Islands provide a protected environment for snakes to thrive without the presence of major predators such as large mammals or other snake species.

# 185.

The Galapagos Islands are a popular destination for wildlife enthusiasts and nature lovers who are interested in observing unique snake species in their natural habitats.

# 186.

Snakes in the Galapagos Islands have adapted to the distinct climate patterns of the archipelago, which include a dry season and a wet season.

# 187.

The isolation of the Galapagos Islands has allowed for the development of unique behaviors and adaptations in snakes, contributing to their ecological importance.

# 188.

Galapagos snakes are highly dependent on the availability of suitable prey populations, making them vulnerable to changes in the ecosystem caused by human activities or introduced species.

# 189.

Climate change poses a potential threat to the survival of Galapagos snakes, as alterations in temperature and precipitation patterns could impact their habitats and prey availability.

# 190.

Galapagos snakes are considered a valuable component of the overall biodiversity of the archipelago and are protected under Galapagos National Park regulations.

# 191.

The Galapagos National Park implements measures to control the spread of invasive species that may pose a threat to native snakes and their habitats.

# 192.

Galapagos snakes are part of a larger conservation effort to preserve the unique and fragile ecosystem of the Galapagos Islands.

# 193.

Scientific research on Galapagos snakes has contributed to our understanding of evolutionary processes, island biogeography, and the ecological dynamics of the Galapagos Islands.

# 194.

The Galapagos Islands serve as a natural laboratory for studying the adaptation and evolution of snakes in response to environmental challenges.

# 195.

The Galapagos snake species have likely evolved from ancestral populations that colonized the islands by natural dispersal or through accidental transport by human activities.

# 196.

Galapagos snakes are excellent swimmers and are known to cross small channels of water between the islands.

# 197.

Snakes play a crucial role in maintaining the balance of the Galapagos Island ecosystems by controlling populations of prey species and contributing to nutrient cycling.

# 198.

The Galapagos Islands provide a unique opportunity to study the interaction between snakes and other endemic species, such as the Galapagos tortoise and marine iguanas.

# 199.

The conservation efforts focused on protecting Galapagos snakes are part of a broader initiative to preserve the unique biodiversity of the Galapagos Islands.

# 200.

The presence of Galapagos snakes is a testament to the remarkable adaptive processes that have shaped the fauna of the archipelago and make them a fascinating component of the Galapagos ecosystem.

# 201.

Lowe's Companies, Inc., commonly known as Lowe's, was founded in 1946 by Lucius Smith Lowe in North Wilkesboro, North Carolina, USA.

# 202.

The first Lowe's store was a small hardware store that primarily sold hardware and appliances.

# 203.

Lowe's was initially a local store, but it expanded rapidly and became a regional retailer in the 1950s.

# 204.

In the 1960s, Lowe's began to open stores outside of North Carolina, expanding its reach to neighboring states.

# 205.

Lowe's went public in 1961 and became listed on the New York Stock Exchange.

# 206.

The company's growth accelerated in the 1970s, with the acquisition of several regional hardware chains.

# 207.

In 1982, Lowe's reached the milestone of 100 stores across the United States.

# 208.

Lowe's expanded its product offerings beyond hardware and appliances, including adding home improvement products like lumber, flooring, and paint.

# 209.

In the 1990s, Lowe's continued its expansion, opening stores in new markets across the country.

# 210.

The 1990s also saw Lowe's introduce its "Everyday Low Prices" strategy, which aimed to provide competitive pricing on a wide range of products.

# 211.

Lowe's established a presence in the international market by opening its first store in Canada in 2007.

# 212.

In 2010, Lowe's acquired the 72-store chain, ATG Stores, expanding its online retail presence.

# 213.

The company launched its online store, lowes.com, in 1996, offering customers the convenience of shopping from home.

# 214.

Lowe's has a strong commitment to customer service and aims to provide a helpful and knowledgeable shopping experience.

# 215.

Lowe's has a significant focus on sustainability and has implemented numerous initiatives to reduce its environmental impact.

## 216.

The company operates several LEED-certified stores, demonstrating its commitment to energy efficiency and sustainable building practices.

## 217.

Lowe's established the Lowe's Charitable and Educational Foundation, which supports community projects and provides grants to schools and nonprofit organizations.

## 218.

In 2006, Lowe's introduced the "MyLowes" program, which allows customers to create an online profile to manage their purchases, track warranties, and access personalized project ideas.

## 219.

Lowe's has been recognized with various awards for its corporate responsibility efforts, including being named one of the World's Most Ethical Companies by Ethisphere.

## 220.

The company has a strong presence in the home improvement industry, competing with other major retailers like The Home Depot.

## 221.

Lowe's operates a distribution network consisting of regional distribution centers and specialized fulfillment centers.

## 222.

In recent years, Lowe's has invested in technology and digital innovation to enhance the customer experience, including the introduction of augmented reality and virtual reality tools.

## 223.

Lowe's sponsors NASCAR driver Jimmie Johnson, who has won seven championships, and has a long-standing partnership with the racing industry.

## 224.

Lowe's has a significant commitment to diversity and inclusion, fostering an inclusive work environment and supporting initiatives that promote equality.

## 225.

The company has a strong presence on social media platforms, engaging with customers and providing DIY tips, inspiration, and project ideas.

## 226.

Lowe's has a dedicated team of employees known as Lowe's Heroes who volunteer their time to assist with community projects and disaster relief efforts.

## 227.

The company has a comprehensive training program for its employees, providing ongoing development opportunities and promoting a culture of learning.

## 228.

Lowe's operates various store formats, including large-format stores, neighborhood stores, and specialized stores focused on specific product categories.

## 229.

The company has expanded its product offerings to include appliances, outdoor living products, flooring, and kitchen and bath fixtures.

## 230.

Lowe's has a Price Match Guarantee, ensuring customers get the best prices on comparable products.

## 231.

Lowe's offers installation services for various products, including flooring, windows, and appliances, providing customers with a one-stop shopping experience.

## 232.

The company has a strong online presence, offering customers the option to shop online, schedule deliveries, and access a wide range of resources and tutorials.

## 233.

Lowe's has a dedicated Pro Services division that caters to professional contractors, offering specialized services and discounts.

## 234.

The company actively supports and promotes DIY culture through workshops, classes, and online tutorials, empowering customers to tackle their home improvement projects.

## 235.

Lowe's has a commitment to sustainability and has set goals to reduce carbon emissions, increase energy efficiency, and promote responsible sourcing.

## 236.

The company has a dedicated team of experts known as the Lowe's Innovation Labs, focused on developing innovative products and technologies for the home improvement industry.

## 237.

Lowe's has been recognized as a top employer, offering competitive benefits, advancement opportunities, and a positive work environment.

## 238.

The company has been involved in disaster relief efforts, providing support and supplies to affected communities during natural disasters.

## 239.

Lowe's has been recognized for its philanthropic efforts, donating millions of dollars to charitable organizations and disaster relief initiatives.

## 240.

The company has a dedicated customer loyalty program called "Lowe's Advantage," offering members exclusive benefits, discounts, and personalized offers.

## 241.

Lowe's has a strong commitment to safe and sustainable product offerings, ensuring compliance with regulations and promoting eco-friendly choices.

## 242.

The company actively supports veteran hiring initiatives and has committed to hiring 20,000veterans by 2025.

## 243.

Lowe's has a partnership with Habitat for Humanity, providing volunteer support and materials for building affordable housing.

## 244.

The company has a comprehensive supplier diversity program, supporting small and diverse businesses and promoting inclusion in its supply chain.

# 245.

Lowe's has a strong presence in social media advertising, utilizing platforms like Facebook, Instagram, and YouTube to reach and engage with customers.

# 246.

The company has a mobile app that allows customers to shop, track orders, and access personalized recommendations.

# 247.

Lowe's has a commitment to accessibility, ensuring its stores and online platforms are inclusive and accessible to people with disabilities.

# 248.

The company has implemented various initiatives to enhance the safety and well-being of its employees and customers, particularly during the COVID-19 pandemic.

# 249.

Lowe's has received recognition for its employee volunteerism and community engagement, including being named one of the Civic 50 companies for corporate social responsibility.

# 250.

Throughout its history, Lowe's has remained dedicated to its founding principles of providing quality products, excellent customer service, and a commitment to improving homes and communities.

# 251.

Bloomberg L.P., commonly known as Bloomberg, was founded by Michael Bloomberg in 1981.

## 252.

Michael Bloomberg initially started the company to provide financial data and information to Wall Street professionals.

## 253.

The first product launched by Bloomberg was the Bloomberg Terminal, a computer software system that provides real-time financial data and analytics.

## 254.

Bloomberg Terminal quickly became a widely used tool in the financial industry, providing traders, analysts, and investors with access to market data, news, and analysis.

## 255.

In addition to financial data, Bloomberg expanded its services to include news, research, and media through various platforms.

## 256.

Bloomberg News, the company's news division, was launched in 1990 and has grown to become a leading global news organization, providing business and financial news across different industries.

## 257.

Bloomberg's news coverage is known for its extensive financial reporting, analysis, and investigative journalism.

## 258.

Bloomberg News operates with a global network of journalists and has offices in major cities around the world.

259.

Bloomberg's media division expanded to include television, radio, and digital platforms, reaching a wide audience with business and financial news coverage.

260.

Bloomberg Television provides 24-hour news coverage, including interviews with prominent business leaders and influential figures.

261.

Bloomberg Radio offers live news broadcasts and analysis, with a focus on business and finance.

262.

Bloomberg's digital platforms, including the Bloomberg website and mobile apps, provide users with access to real-time news, market data, and financial tools.

263.

Bloomberg's media platforms are known for their objective reporting and nonpartisan coverage of business and financial news.

264.

Bloomberg LP operates various businesses beyond news and media, including Bloomberg Intelligence, Bloomberg Law, and Bloomberg Government.

265.

Bloomberg Intelligence provides in-depth research and analysis across industries, helping investors and professionals make informed decisions.

266.

Bloomberg Law is a legal research platform that offers access to legal content, news, and analysis.

## 267.

Bloomberg Government provides information and analysis on government policies, regulations, and legislative activities.

## 268.

Bloomberg LP has expanded its services to include enterprise software solutions for financial professionals, offering data management, analytics, and trading platforms.

## 269.

Bloomberg LP is known for its commitment to data accuracy and quality, providing reliable financial and market data to its users.

## 270.

Bloomberg LP has a strong presence in financial markets globally, serving clients in the banking, investment, and corporate sectors.

## 271.

The company's success has allowed Bloomberg to become one of the wealthiest individuals in the world, with Michael Bloomberg consistently appearing on lists of the richest people globally.

## 272.

Bloomberg LP has a strong corporate culture focused on innovation, integrity, and collaboration.

## 273.

The company is known for its open-office layout and a collaborative work environment that encourages idea-sharing and teamwork.

## 274.

Bloomberg LP has received numerous awards and accolades for its products, services, and workplace culture.

## 275.

Bloomberg LP has a global footprint, with offices and operations in major financial centers around the world.

## 276.

Bloomberg LP has made significant investments in technology and data infrastructure to support its extensive product offerings.

## 277.

The company's commitment to sustainability led to the construction of Bloomberg's headquarters in New York City, which is one of the most environmentally friendly buildings in the world.

## 278.

Bloomberg Philanthropies, the philanthropic arm of Bloomberg LP, supports various causes and initiatives globally, including public health, the environment, education, and the arts.

## 279.

Michael Bloomberg served as the Mayor of New York City for three terms from 2002 to 2013 and used his business experience and resources to tackle issues such as public health, education, and sustainability.

## 280.

Bloomberg LP has a strong emphasis on diversity and inclusion, actively promoting a diverse workforce and fostering an inclusive work environment.

## 281.

The company has been recognized for its efforts in promoting gender equality and women's leadership, with initiatives such as the Bloomberg Gender-Equality Index.

## 282.

Bloomberg LP has been at the forefront of leveraging data and technology in the financial industry, pioneering new approaches to data analysis and market insights.

## 283.

The Bloomberg Terminal has become an essential tool for financial professionals, with thousands of subscribers worldwide relying on its data and analytics.

## 284.

Bloomberg LP has expanded its coverage beyond traditional financial markets to include areas such as environmental, social, and governance (ESG) investing.

## 285.

The company has been a strong advocate for transparency and accountability in financial markets, pushing for increased regulation and improved data standards.

## 286.

Bloomberg LP has been involved in various philanthropic initiatives aimed at improving global public health, including the Bloomberg Initiative to Reduce Tobacco Use.

## 287.

Bloomberg LP has a strong focus on corporate social responsibility, supporting employee volunteerism and contributing to social and environmental causes.

## 288.

The company has a comprehensive Code of Conduct and Ethics, promoting integrity, transparency, and responsible business practices.

## 289.

Bloomberg LP has a long history of supporting journalism and press freedom, with Bloomberg News reporters covering critical stories and breaking news globally.

## 290.

Bloomberg LP has expanded its offerings to include specialized products for different industries, such as BloombergNEF for renewable energy and Bloomberg Law for legal professionals.

## 291.

The company has invested in advanced technology, including artificial intelligence and machine learning, to enhance its data analytics capabilities.

## 292.

Bloomberg LP has received recognition for its workplace culture and employee satisfaction, appearing on lists of top employers globally.

## 293.

Bloomberg LP has been active in supporting initiatives to address climate change and promote sustainable business practices.

## 294.

The company has established partnerships with organizations and governments to promote data-driven decision-making and policy development.

## 295.

Bloomberg LP has been an advocate for diversity in the workplace and has implemented programs and initiatives to increase representation and inclusivity.

## 296.

The Bloomberg Terminal has evolved over time, incorporating new features and tools to meet the changing needs of the financial industry.

## 297.

Bloomberg LP has a strong commitment to data privacy and security, implementing robust measures to protect user information and prevent unauthorized access.

## 298.

The company has a dedicated customer support team that provides assistance to Bloomberg Terminal users and ensures smooth operation and user satisfaction.

## 299.

Bloomberg LP continues to innovate and expand its product offerings, adapting to the evolving needs of the financial industry and its users.

## 300.

Bloomberg LP has established itself as a global leader in providing financial data, news, and analysis, and its impact on the financial industry is significant.

## 301.

Denver Civic Center is a historic civic center located in downtown Denver, Colorado.

## 302.

The Civic Center was designed by renowned architect Charles Mulford Robinson and completed in 1910.

## 303.

The Civic Center was intended to be the cultural and governmental center of Denver, featuring grand buildings and public spaces.

## 304.

The centerpiece of the Civic Center is the Civic Center Park, spanning 12.5 acres and offering a green oasis in the heart of the city.

## 305.

The park features beautifully landscaped gardens, walking paths, and numerous statues and monuments.

## 306.

The park is home to the iconic Greek Amphitheater, an open-air theater used for concerts and performances.

## 307.

At the center of the park is the Voorhies Memorial, a striking marble monument honoring the Colorado soldiers who fought in the Spanish-American War.

## 308.

The park hosts numerous events throughout the year, including cultural festivals, art exhibitions, and community gatherings.

## 309.

Surrounding the park are several significant buildings, including the Denver City and County Building.

## 310.

The Denver City and County Building is a stunning neoclassical
building completed in 1932 and serves as the seat of city
government.

# 311.

The building is known for its distinctive gold dome, which is made
of real gold leaf.

# 312.

The Civic Center also houses the Colorado State Capitol, an iconic
building with its distinctive golden dome.

# 313.

The Colorado State Capitol is where the state's legislative and
executive branches are housed.

# 314.

The Capitol building sits at exactly one mile above sea level, earning
Denver the nickname "The Mile High City."

# 315.

The Capitol features beautiful architectural details, including stained
glass windows, murals, and a grand staircase.

# 316.

The grounds of the Civic Center are adorned with several impressive
statues and sculptures, honoring notable figures from Colorado's
history.

# 317.

One of the most famous statues is the "The American Indian" by
Alexander Phimister Proctor, which stands at the southern end of the
park.

## 318.

The "The American Indian" statue pays tribute to the Native American tribes that once inhabited the region.

## 319.

The Civic Center is also home to the Denver Art Museum, located just south of the park.

## 320.

The Denver Art Museum is known for its diverse collection of art, including Native American, Western, and contemporary works.

## 321.

The museum building itself is an architectural marvel, with a unique design inspired by the region's natural landscape.

## 322.

Adjacent to the Denver Art Museum is the Clyfford Still Museum, dedicated to the life and works of renowned abstract expressionist painter Clyfford Still.

## 323.

The Civic Center is a popular spot for public events and celebrations, including Independence Day fireworks, parades, and cultural festivals.

## 324.

The Civic Center is also known for its lively food truck scene, with various food trucks regularly parked around the park, offering a wide range of cuisines.

## 325.

The Civic Center is a designated National Historic Landmark, recognizing its historical and cultural significance.

# 326.

The Civic Center has undergone various revitalization efforts to preserve its historic buildings and enhance its public spaces.

# 327.

In 2012, the Denver Civic Center was designated as a Denver Landmark, ensuring its protection and preservation for future generations.

# 328.

The Civic Center's architecture and design reflect the City Beautiful movement, which emphasized grand civic spaces and classical architectural styles.

# 329.

The Civic Center is surrounded by important cultural institutions, including the Denver Public Library and the History Colorado Center.

# 330.

The Denver Public Library, located just east of the park, is a modern architectural marvel and serves as a hub of knowledge and learning for the community.

# 331.

The History Colorado Center, located on the west side of the park, offers interactive exhibits and educational programs that showcase the state's rich history.

# 332.

The Civic Center is well-connected to the rest of Denver through its proximity to major roads, public transportation, and bike lanes.

# 333.

The Civic Center hosts the annual Civic Center EATS, a popular food truck festival that brings together a variety of local food vendors.

# 334.

The Civic Center serves as a gathering place for protests, rallies, and demonstrations, allowing people to exercise their right to free speech and assembly.

# 335.

The Civic Center offers stunning views of the surrounding Rocky Mountains, providing a picturesque backdrop for events and leisure activities.

# 336.

The Civic Center is a vibrant and inclusive space that welcomes people of all ages and backgrounds.

# 337.

The Civic Center has been the site of numerous historic moments, including presidential visits, political rallies, and cultural celebrations.

# 338.

The Civic Center is often referred to as the "heart" of Denver, as it symbolizes the city's civic pride and community spirit.

# 339.

The Civic Center has inspired artists, writers, and photographers throughout its history, serving as a muse for creative expression.

# 340.

The Civic Center is a popular destination for locals and tourists alike, offering a blend of historical significance, cultural attractions, and natural beauty.

## 341.

The Civic Center is an important venue for outdoor concerts, with its spacious park and amphitheater providing a scenic backdrop for performances.

## 342.

The Civic Center has been the site of various public art installations, adding an element of creativity and intrigue to the park's landscape.

## 343.

The Civic Center's proximity to the Colorado Convention Center makes it a convenient location for visitors attending conferences and events.

## 344.

The Civic Center has been featured in numerous films and television shows, showcasing its iconic architecture and scenic surroundings.

## 345.

The Civic Center plays a vital role in civic engagement, with public meetings, forums, and community events held within its grounds.

## 346.

The Civic Center's architecture and design have influenced urban planning and development in Denver and beyond.

## 347.

The Civic Center is a popular spot for outdoor recreation, with its expansive lawns, walking paths, and open spaces offering opportunities for picnicking, jogging, and relaxation.

## 348.

The Civic Center has been recognized for its historical and architectural significance by various preservation organizations.

## 349.

The Civic Center provides a peaceful retreat from the hustle and bustle of city life, offering a tranquil oasis in the heart of downtown Denver.

## 350.

The Civic Center is a testament to the city's commitment to preserving its heritage, fostering a sense of community, and creating a vibrant public space for all to enjoy.

## 351.

The Durango-Silverton Narrow-Gauge Railroad is a historic steam-powered train that operates in southwestern Colorado.

## 352.

The railroad was originally built in 1881 to transport silver and gold ore from the San Juan Mountains to the town of Durango.

## 353.

The train runs along a narrow-gauge track, which is only three feet wide, making it one of the few remaining narrow-gauge railroads in the United States.

## 354.

The Durango-Silverton Narrow-Gauge Railroad covers a distance of 45 miles, taking passengers on a scenic journey through the breathtaking canyons and mountains of the San Juan National Forest.

## 355.

The train route offers stunning views of the Animas River and the surrounding wilderness, providing passengers with a unique perspective of the region's natural beauty.

## 356.

The steam locomotives used on the Durango-Silverton Narrow-Gauge Railroad are historic and have been meticulously preserved to maintain their authenticity.

## 357.

The locomotives are fueled by coal and require daily maintenance and servicing to keep them in working order.

## 358.

The train cars used on the railroad are also historic and have been restored to reflect the style and ambiance of the late 19th century.

## 359.

Passengers have the option to choose between open-air gondola cars or enclosed coaches, each offering a different experience during the journey.

## 360.

The Durango-Silverton Narrow-Gauge Railroad is a popular tourist attraction, drawing visitors from around the world who come to experience its nostalgic charm and scenic beauty.

## 361.

The train operates year-round, with different seasonal experiences for passengers to enjoy.

## 362.

During the summer months, the train offers daily trips, while in the winter, it operates as the Polar Express, a special holiday-themed experience for families.

## 363.

The journey on the Durango-Silverton Narrow-Gauge Railroad is not just a scenic ride but also a historical and educational experience.

## 364.

Narrators on board provide passengers with interesting facts and stories about the history of the railroad, the surrounding landscape, and the mining era.

## 365.

The railroad played a significant role in the mining industry of the region, transporting tons of ore from the mountains to the smelters in Durango.

## 366.

The construction of the railroad was a monumental engineering feat, involving the carving of narrow ledges into the sides of cliffs and the construction of high trestles.

## 367.

The train route includes several notable landmarks, such as the High Line, a section of track that hugs the mountainside at a significant elevation.

## 368.

The railroad is known for its "rockfall alley," where passengers can witness the remnants of past rockslides that have been cleared from the tracks.

## 369.

The Durango-Silverton Narrow-Gauge Railroad has been featured in several movies and television shows, adding to its allure and popularity.

# 370.

The train journey offers a glimpse into the history of the Old West, as the railroad played a crucial role in the development of the region during the mining boom.

# 371.

The Durango-Silverton Narrow-Gauge Railroad is listed on the National Register of Historic Places, recognizing its cultural and historical significance.

# 372.

The railroad is operated by a dedicated team of professionals who have a deep passion for preserving the history and heritage of the region.

# 373.

The Durango-Silverton Narrow-Gauge Railroad offers various excursion options, including half-day trips, full-day trips, and special event trains.

# 374.

The train departs from the historic depot in downtown Durango, which has been beautifully restored to its original 1882 appearance.

# 375.

The depot houses a museum where visitors can learn more about the history of the railroad and the impact it had on the local community.

# 376.

The Durango-Silverton Narrow-Gauge Railroad has been recognized as one of the most scenic train rides in the United States.

# 377.

The train journey takes passengers through remote and inaccessible areas of the San Juan National Forest, offering a unique perspective on the untouched wilderness.

## 378.

The railroad has strict safety protocols in place to ensure the well-being of passengers and staff, including regular inspections of the tracks and equipment.

## 379.

The Durango-Silverton Narrow-Gauge Railroad has withstood the test of time and remains an iconic symbol of Colorado's rich mining and railroad history.

## 380.

The train ride is a favorite among photographers, as it provides countless opportunities for capturing stunning landscapes and dramatic vistas.

## 381.

The railroad hosts special events throughout the year, such as wine and beer tastings, music concerts, and holiday-themed excursions.

## 382.

The Durango-Silverton Narrow-Gauge Railroad has been featured in several travel publications and guidebooks as a must-visit attraction in Colorado.

## 383.

The train journey is not just a mode of transportation but a step back in time, allowing passengers to experience the sights, sounds, and smells of a bygone era.

## 384.

The train's steam whistle has become an iconic sound associated with the railroad, creating a nostalgic atmosphere during the journey.

## 385.

The Durango-Silverton Narrow-Gauge Railroad has a dedicated fan base of train enthusiasts who appreciate the authenticity and historical significance of the railroad.

## 386.

The railroad offers special packages and discounts for families, groups, and individuals, making it accessible to a wide range of visitors.

## 387.

The journey on the Durango-Silverton Narrow-Gauge Railroad is an immersive experience that transports passengers to a different era, evoking a sense of adventure and exploration.

## 388.

The train route passes through pristine mountain streams, dense forests, and towering peaks, providing a serene and awe-inspiring backdrop for the journey.

## 389.

The railroad has received numerous awards and accolades for its preservation efforts, tourism impact, and commitment to providing a unique visitor experience.

## 390.

The Durango-Silverton Narrow-Gauge Railroad has become an integral part of the local community, supporting local businesses and contributing to the region's economy.

## 391.

The train ride is a popular choice for special occasions, such as weddings, anniversaries, and family reunions, offering a memorable and picturesque setting for celebrations.

## 392.

The railroad offers various add-on experiences, such as guided hikes, wildlife tours, and photography workshops, allowing passengers to further explore the natural beauty of the region.

## 393.

The train's vintage steam locomotives have been featured in several historical reenactments and celebrations, bringing the past to life for spectators.

## 394.

The Durango-Silverton Narrow-Gauge Railroad has inspired artists, writers, and filmmakers, who have captured its timeless beauty and historic significance in their works.

## 395.

The railroad has a gift shop where visitors can purchase souvenirs, memorabilia, and train-related merchandise.

## 396.

The Durango-Silverton Narrow-Gauge Railroad has been recognized for its commitment to sustainability and environmental stewardship, implementing practices to minimize its carbon footprint.

## 397.

The train journey provides a unique opportunity to disconnect from the modern world and immerse oneself in the simplicity and charm of a bygone era.

## 398.

The Durango-Silverton Narrow-Gauge Railroad is an enduring symbol of the American West, evoking images of pioneers, prospectors, and the rugged frontier spirit.

## 399.

The railroad has a strong presence in the local tourism industry, attracting visitors from across the country and around the world to experience its historic allure.

## 400.

The Durango-Silverton Narrow-Gauge Railroad continues to preserve and celebrate the heritage of Colorado's mining and railroad history, providing a remarkable and unforgettable experience for all who embark on its journey.

## 401.

The Galapagos Sperm Whale (Physeter macrocephalus) is the largest toothed whale species and one of the largest predators in the world.

## 402.

Adult male sperm whales can reach lengths of up to 60 feet (18 meters) and weigh around 45-50 tons.

## 403.

The Galapagos Sperm Whale has a distinctive body shape, with a massive, square-shaped head and a long, narrow lower jaw.

## 404.

The head of a sperm whale accounts for about one-third of its total body length and houses a large spermaceti organ filled with a waxy substance called spermaceti.

## 405.

The spermaceti organ helps regulate the whale's buoyancy by changing the density of the oil inside it.

# 406.

Sperm whales have the largest brains of any animal on Earth, weighing an average of 17 pounds (7.8 kilograms).

# 407.

The Galapagos Sperm Whale has a dark gray or brownish body color with a wrinkled appearance caused by large, overlapping skin folds.

# 408.

Sperm whales have a single blowhole located on the left side of their head, which creates a distinctive bushy blow when they surface to breathe.

# 409.

The Galapagos Sperm Whale is known for its deep-diving abilities and can reach depths of over 3,280 feet (1,000 meters) in search of prey.

# 410.

Sperm whales primarily feed on large squid, but they also consume fish and occasionally other marine mammals.

# 411.

The Galapagos Sperm Whale has a unique hunting strategy called "drift diving," where it dives vertically down and then drifts horizontally in search of prey.

# 412.

Sperm whales have a specialized echolocation system that allows them to locate prey in the darkness of the deep ocean using sound waves.

# 413.

The vocalizations of sperm whales, known as "clicks," are some of the loudest sounds produced by any animal and can be heard underwater for miles.

# 414.

Sperm whales are highly social animals and live in family groups called "pods." The pod is typically led by a dominant female known as the matriarch.

# 415.

The Galapagos Sperm Whale pod consists of adult females, their offspring, and occasionally juvenile males.

# 416.

Male sperm whales typically live solitary lives or form smaller bachelor groups away from the main pods.

# 417.

Sperm whales are known for their complex social behaviors and vocalizations, which are believed to play a role in communication and social bonding.

# 418.

The breeding season for Galapagos Sperm Whales occurs during the cooler months, and mating takes place in tropical or subtropical waters.

# 419.

The gestation period for sperm whales is approximately 14-16 months, and females give birth to a single calf, which is about 13-16 feet (4-5 meters) long at birth.

# 420.

Newborn sperm whales are often protected and cared for by other females in the pod, known as "aunts."

## 421.

The Galapagos Sperm Whale calf depends on its mother's milk for nourishment, and it can consume up to 500 liters of milk per day.

## 422.

The calves stay with their mothers for several years, learning essential survival skills and social behaviors.

## 423.

The Galapagos Sperm Whale has a lifespan of around 70 years, with females generally outliving males.

## 424.

Sperm whales have been historically targeted by whalers for their valuable oil, blubber, and spermaceti, which were used in various industries.

## 425.

The global population of sperm whales has declined significantly due to past commercial whaling, but they are now protected by international laws and regulations.

## 426.

The Galapagos Sperm Whale population is relatively stable and benefits from the protection provided by the Galapagos Marine Reserve.

## 427.

Sperm whales are considered a "keystone species" in the marine ecosystem, as they have a significant influence on the structure and dynamics of their habitat.

## 428.

The large quantities of fecal matter produced by sperm whales contribute to nutrient cycling in the ocean, supporting the growth of phytoplankton and other marine organisms.

## 429.

Sperm whales play a crucial role in carbon sequestration by storing carbon dioxide in their bodies and depositing it on the ocean floor when they die.

## 430.

The Galapagos Sperm Whale is one of the iconic species found in the Galapagos Islands and contributes to the archipelago's unique marine biodiversity.

## 431.

The Galapagos Sperm Whale can often be observed in the waters surrounding the Galapagos Islands, particularly around the deep underwater canyons.

## 432.

Sperm whales are curious and have been known to approach boats, providing unique opportunities for up-close encounters with these majestic creatures.

## 433.

The Galapagos Sperm Whale is protected by the Galapagos National Park regulations, which prohibit harassment or disturbance of the animals.

## 434.

Researchers study Galapagos Sperm Whales to gain insights into their behavior, population dynamics, and ecological role in the marine environment.

## 435.

The study of sperm whales has contributed to scientific understanding of deep-sea ecosystems, acoustic communication, and social structures in cetaceans.

## 436.

Sperm whale vocalizations have been the subject of extensive research and have even inspired musicians and artists.

## 437.

The Galapagos Sperm Whale is part of a complex marine ecosystem in the Galapagos Islands, interacting with other species such as dolphins, sharks, and seabirds.

## 438.

The presence of sperm whales in the Galapagos Marine Reserve is an indicator of the area's health and productivity.

## 439.

The conservation of the Galapagos Sperm Whale is essential for maintaining the overall balance and ecological integrity of the marine environment in the Galapagos Islands.

## 440.

Galapagos Sperm Whales contribute to the ecotourism industry in the Galapagos Islands, attracting visitors from around the world who wish to witness these magnificent creatures in their natural habitat.

## 441.

Galapagos Sperm Whales have been the subject of documentaries and scientific studies, which have helped raise awareness about their importance and conservation status.

## 442.

The Galapagos Islands provide a unique research opportunity to study the behavior and population dynamics of Galapagos Sperm Whales in a protected and relatively undisturbed environment.

## 443.

Efforts are underway to develop conservation strategies and management plans to ensure the long-term survival of Galapagos Sperm Whales and their habitat.

## 444.

The Galapagos Sperm Whale serves as a flagship species for marine conservation in the Galapagos Islands, representing the need to protect the entire marine ecosystem.

## 445.

Public awareness campaigns and educational programs are conducted to inform visitors and residents about the importance of conservation and responsible wildlife viewing practices.

## 446.

The Galapagos Sperm Whale symbolizes the rich biodiversity and natural heritage of the Galapagos Islands, contributing to their status as a UNESCO World Heritage Site.

## 447.

The study and conservation of Galapagos Sperm Whales contribute to the broader understanding of marine ecosystems and the need for global efforts to protect and preserve our oceans.

## 448.

Galapagos Sperm Whales have inspired awe and fascination in people for centuries, with their immense size, intelligence, and unique adaptations.

## 449.

The Galapagos Sperm Whale represents the fragile balance between human activities and the natural world, highlighting the importance of sustainable practices and conservation efforts.

# 450.

The presence of Galapagos Sperm Whales in the waters of the Galapagos Islands is a reminder of the interconnectedness of all life forms and the responsibility we have to protect and conserve the natural world for future generations. The Galapagos Sperm Whale is a majestic and iconic species that continues to captivate and inspire awe, reminding us of the beauty and wonder of our oceans and the need to preserve them.

# 451.

The Galapagos Storm Petrel (Oceanodroma tethys) is a small seabird species that is endemic to the Galapagos Islands.

# 452.

They are part of the Procellariiformes order, commonly known as tube-nosed seabirds.

# 453.

Galapagos Storm Petrels are primarily nocturnal, spending most of their time at sea and returning to the islands only to breed.

# 454.

They have a unique and distinctive flight pattern, with rapid wingbeats and a buoyant flight style.

# 455.

These birds have a dark brown to black plumage, which helps them blend in with the dark ocean waters when seen from above.

# 456.

The Galapagos Storm Petrel has a white rump and a narrow, deeply forked tail.

## 457.

They have a small, hooked beak that is well-suited for catching and feeding on small fish and squid.

## 458.

These birds are highly adapted to life at sea and have a gland above their nasal passage that helps remove excess salt from their bodies.

## 459.

Galapagos Storm Petrels are known for their remarkable ability to navigate and find their way back to their nesting sites in complete darkness.

## 460.

The nesting sites of Galapagos Storm Petrels are typically found in rocky crevices and cliffs on the Galapagos Islands.

## 461.

They form large breeding colonies, often nesting in close proximity to other seabird species.

## 462.

The breeding season for Galapagos Storm Petrels usually occurs from January to May.

## 463.

Female Galapagos Storm Petrels lay a single egg, which is incubated by both parents for about 40 days.

## 464.

The parents take turns incubating the egg and foraging at sea to bring back food for their chick.

## 465.

The chicks hatch with a downy plumage and are initially helpless, relying on their parents for food and protection.

## 466.

After a few weeks, the chicks develop flight feathers and are able to fledge from their nests.

## 467.

Galapagos Storm Petrels have a high chick mortality rate due to predation from introduced species such as rats and cats.

## 468.

They are also vulnerable to disturbances caused by human activities and climate change.

## 469.

Galapagos Storm Petrels are skilled divers and can plunge into the ocean from great heights to catch their prey.

## 470.

They feed on a diet primarily composed of small fish, squid, and crustaceans.

## 471.

Galapagos Storm Petrels are known to follow fishing boats and feed on discarded fish and other food scraps.

## 472.

These birds have a unique vocalization, which consists of a series of high-pitched whistles and trills.

# 473.

The calls of Galapagos Storm Petrels are often used for communication and locating their mates and chicks in the dark.

# 474.

They have a lifespan of around 10-15 years.

# 475.

Galapagos Storm Petrels are not strong fliers and are more adapted for maneuvering and gliding close to the water's surface.

# 476.

They are agile swimmers and use their wings to propel themselves underwater in search of prey.

# 477.

Galapagos Storm Petrels are an important part of the marine ecosystem, as they help control populations of small fish and squid.

# 478.

The population size of Galapagos Storm Petrels is currently unknown, but they are considered to be a species of least concern according to the IUCN Red List.

# 479.

These birds are protected within the Galapagos Marine Reserve and their nesting sites are closely monitored to prevent disturbances.

# 480.

Galapagos Storm Petrels are known to migrate long distances between their breeding sites in the Galapagos Islands and their feeding grounds in the eastern Pacific Ocean.

# 481.

They are highly sensitive to changes in oceanic conditions and their distribution may be influenced by factors such as sea surface temperature and availability of prey.

# 482.

Galapagos Storm Petrels are solitary foragers, often traveling long distances in search of food.

# 483.

They have been observed traveling up to 80 kilometers (50 miles) from their breeding sites to find food.

# 484.

Galapagos Storm Petrels play a role in nutrient cycling, as their droppings contribute to the fertilization of the surrounding marine ecosystem.

# 485.

These birds are important indicators of the health and productivity of the marine environment in the Galapagos Islands.

# 486.

Their population dynamics and foraging behavior provide valuable insights into the state of the local marine ecosystem.

# 487.

Galapagos Storm Petrels are occasionally preyed upon by larger seabirds such as the Galapagos Hawk and the Lava Gull.

# 488.

They have a cryptic nesting behavior, often choosing hidden crevices and burrows to protect their eggs and chicks from predators.

# 489.

Galapagos Storm Petrels are not commonly seen by visitors to the Galapagos Islands, as they spend most of their lives at sea.

# 490.

Efforts are underway to monitor and study the population trends and ecological significance of Galapagos Storm Petrels in the Galapagos Islands.

# 491.

Researchers use techniques such as satellite tracking and genetic analysis to better understand the migratory patterns and genetic diversity of these birds.

# 492.

Galapagos Storm Petrels have captivated the interest of birdwatchers and researchers who visit the Galapagos Islands in search of rare and endemic species.

# 493.

The Galapagos Islands provide a unique opportunity to study the behavior and ecology of Galapagos Storm Petrels in their natural habitat.

# 494.

The conservation of Galapagos Storm Petrels is crucial for maintaining the biodiversity and ecological balance of the Galapagos Marine Reserve.

# 495.

Educational programs and awareness campaigns are conducted to educate visitors and local communities about the importance of protecting Galapagos Storm Petrels and their habitats.

## 496.

The study of Galapagos Storm Petrels contributes to our understanding of seabird ecology, migration patterns, and the impacts of climate change on marine species.

## 497.

These birds have a captivating beauty and grace, with their swift flight and unique adaptations to life at sea.

## 498.

The Galapagos Storm Petrel is a living testament to the incredible diversity and evolutionary processes that have shaped the Galapagos Islands.

## 499.

The presence of Galapagos Storm Petrels in the Galapagos Islands reminds us of the delicate balance between human activities and the natural world.

## 500.

Protecting the Galapagos Storm Petrel and its habitat is essential for preserving the unique biodiversity and ecological integrity of the Galapagos Islands for future generations.

## 501.

KFC, which stands for Kentucky Fried Chicken, was founded by Harland Sanders in 1952 in North Corbin, Kentucky, United States.

## 502.

Harland Sanders, also known as Colonel Sanders, was a successful businessman and a famous figure in the fast food industry.

## 503.

The original KFC restaurant was a small roadside establishment called "Sanders Court & Café," where Sanders served his famous fried chicken recipe.

## 504.

The secret recipe for KFC's fried chicken, which includes a blend of 11 herbs and spices, was developed by Colonel Sanders and remains a closely guarded secret to this day.

## 505.

The popularity of Sanders' fried chicken grew rapidly, leading to the expansion of KFC through franchising.

## 506.

The first KFC franchise was opened in 1952 in Salt Lake City, Utah.

## 507.

KFC's distinctive red and white striped packaging, as well as its iconic logo featuring Colonel Sanders, became recognizable symbols of the brand.

## 508.

In 1957, the Kentucky Fried Chicken Corporation was established, and its headquarters were located in Louisville, Kentucky.

## 509.

KFC's expansion continued throughout the 1960s, with franchises opening across the United States and even internationally.

## 510.

KFC became known for its innovative marketing strategies, including the use of catchy slogans such as "Finger-Lickin' Good" and memorable advertising campaigns.

# 511.

In 1964, KFC was acquired by a group of investors led by John Y. Brown Jr. and Jack C. Massey.

# 512.

Under new ownership, KFC experienced significant growth and became a global brand.

# 513.

In 1971, KFC introduced its first-ever international restaurant in Canada.

# 514.

KFC's international expansion continued throughout the 1970s and 1980s, with restaurants opening in various countries around the world.

# 515.

In 1986, KFC was acquired by PepsiCo, a multinational food and beverage corporation.

# 516.

The merger with PepsiCo allowed KFC to benefit from its vast resources and distribution networks, further accelerating its global growth.

# 517.

In the 1990s, KFC expanded its menu to include a variety of new products, such as chicken sandwiches, wraps, and salads, in response to changing consumer preferences.

# 518.

KFC's success led to the establishment of numerous iconic restaurant designs, including the "bucket-shaped" restaurants that became synonymous with the brand.

# 519.

KFC has a strong presence in China, where it is one of the most popular fast food chains. The first KFC restaurant in China opened in Beijing in 1987.

# 520.

KFC is known for its commitment to social responsibility and community involvement. The company has supported various charitable initiatives and organizations worldwide.

# 521.

KFC has been involved in several philanthropic efforts, including the KFC Colonel's Scholars Program, which provides scholarships to deserving students.

# 522.

In 1991, KFC launched the "Buckets for the Cure" campaign, raising funds for breast cancer research and awareness.

# 523.

KFC has faced various controversies and challenges throughout its history. One notable controversy was the transition from using the term "Kentucky Fried Chicken" to the acronym "KFC" in the 1990s, which sparked rumors and misinformation about the quality of the food.

# 524.

In 2002, KFC introduced its popular "I Love You, Colonel Sanders!" advertising campaign, featuring a fictionalized and caricatured version of Colonel Sanders.

## 525.

KFC's menu has continued to evolve, with the introduction of new products and limited-time offerings. Some notable additions include the Double Down, a sandwich with fried chicken patties instead of bread, and the Nashville Hot Chicken.

## 526.

KFC has been recognized as a leader in the fast food industry, receiving numerous awards for its food quality, customer service, and marketing efforts.

## 527.

KFC has been portrayed in popular culture through movies, television shows, and music. The brand's iconic logo and Colonel Sanders character have become symbols of American fast food.

## 528.

KFC has been at the forefront of innovation in the fast food industry, implementing new technologies such as self-service kiosks and mobile ordering to enhance the customer experience.

## 529.

KFC has a strong online presence and engages with customers through social media platforms, allowing for direct interaction and feedback.

## 530.

KFC has embraced sustainability initiatives, such as adopting eco-friendly packaging and implementing energy-saving measures in its restaurants.

## 531.

In recent years, KFC has focused on expanding its vegetarian and vegan offerings, catering to the growing demand for plant-based options.

## 532.

KFC is known for its commitment to quality and food safety. The company ensures that its chicken suppliers adhere to strict standards and practices.

## 533.

KFC has faced challenges related to animal welfare, and the company has made efforts to improve the treatment of animals in its supply chain.

## 534.

KFC has collaborated with various celebrities and influencers to promote its brand and products, including partnerships with musicians, athletes, and actors.

## 535.

KFC's famous slogan, "Finger-Lickin' Good," has become deeply ingrained in popular culture and is recognized worldwide.

## 536.

KFC has been involved in sports sponsorship, including partnerships with professional sports teams and events.

## 537.

The KFC Yum! Center, a sports and entertainment venue located in Louisville, Kentucky, is named after KFC's parent company, Yum! Brands.

## 538.

KFC has embraced digital marketing and advertising campaigns, leveraging online platforms and influencers to engage with a younger audience.

# 539.

KFC's presence in the global fast food market has contributed to its recognition as one of the most iconic and influential fast food brands in the world.

# 540.

KFC operates thousands of restaurants in over 145 countries and territories, making it one of the largest fast food chains globally.

# 541.

KFC's success and popularity have inspired other fast food chains to develop their own fried chicken offerings.

# 542.

KFC has expanded beyond traditional restaurant formats, including drive-thrus, food courts, and delivery services, to cater to the changing needs of consumers.

# 543.

KFC has been recognized for its commitment to diversity and inclusion, promoting equal opportunities within the company and supporting minority-owned businesses.

# 544.

The KFC Foundation, established in 2006, focuses on empowering employees and their families through education, financial assistance, and community outreach.

# 545.

KFC has embraced digital innovation, including mobile ordering apps, delivery partnerships, and loyalty programs, to enhance the customer experience and meet evolving consumer demands.

# 546.

KFC's success has led to the development of other fast food chains under the Yum! Brands umbrella, including Taco Bell and Pizza Hut.

## 547.

KFC has made efforts to reduce its environmental impact by implementing sustainable practices, including waste reduction and energy conservation.

## 548.

KFC has a global supply chain, ensuring the availability and consistency of its products across its vast network of restaurants.

## 549.

KFC has a strong focus on customer satisfaction and regularly seeks feedback to improve its menu offerings and service.

## 550.

The history of KFC is a testament to the entrepreneurial spirit of Colonel Sanders and the brand's commitment to delivering delicious, high-quality fried chicken to customers around the world.

## 551.

DocuSign was founded in 2003 by Tom Gonser, Court Lorenzini, and Eric Ranft in Seattle, Washington, United States.

## 552.

The company's initial focus was on developing electronic signature technology to streamline the process of signing and exchanging documents.

## 553.

DocuSign's first product was released in 2004, allowing users to securely sign documents electronically and eliminating the need for physical signatures and paper documents.

## 554.

The name "DocuSign" was chosen to reflect the company's mission of providing digital solutions for document signing.

## 555.

In 2005, DocuSign received its first patent for its electronic signature technology, establishing its position as a leader in the industry.

## 556.

DocuSign's technology is based on Public Key Infrastructure (PKI), a highly secure encryption system that ensures the integrity and authenticity of electronic signatures.

## 557.

The adoption of DocuSign's electronic signature technology accelerated as businesses recognized the potential for increased efficiency and cost savings.

## 558.

DocuSign quickly expanded its product offerings beyond electronic signatures to include features such as document workflow management, document storage, and integration with popular business software platforms.

## 559.

The company's cloud-based platform allows users to securely access and sign documents from anywhere using a computer or mobile device.

## 560.

In 2010, DocuSign received a significant investment from venture capital firm Kleiner Perkins, further fueling its growth.

# 561.

DocuSign's user base expanded rapidly, with customers ranging from individuals and small businesses to Fortune 500 companies and government organizations.

# 562.

The company played a crucial role in advocating for the legality and acceptance of electronic signatures, working closely with lawmakers and industry organizations.

# 563.

DocuSign's technology complies with international regulations, including the U.S. Electronic Signatures in Global and National Commerce Act (ESIGN) and the European Union's eIDAS Regulation.

# 564.

In 2013, DocuSign secured a funding round of $85 million, valuing the company at over $1 billion and cementing its status as a "unicorn" startup.

# 565.

The growth of mobile devices and the proliferation of smartphones further accelerated DocuSign's adoption, as users could easily sign documents on the go.

# 566.

DocuSign went public in 2018, launching its initial public offering (IPO) on the NASDAQ stock exchange under the ticker symbol "DOCU."

# 567.

The IPO marked a significant milestone for DocuSign and highlighted the increasing demand for digital solutions in the business world.

## 568.

DocuSign continues to innovate and expand its product offerings, introducing features such as advanced analytics, artificial intelligence, and integration with other productivity tools.

## 569.

The company has made strategic acquisitions to enhance its platform capabilities, acquiring companies such as SpringCM, Seal Software, and Liveoak Technologies.

## 570.

DocuSign's global presence extends to over 180 countries, with offices and data centers located around the world.

## 571.

The COVID-19 pandemic further emphasized the need for digital solutions, and DocuSign experienced increased demand as businesses transitioned to remote work and digital document workflows.

## 572.

DocuSign's platform has facilitated the completion of numerous high-profile transactions, including real estate deals, legal agreements, and financial transactions.

## 573.

The company has received numerous awards and recognition for its innovative technology and positive impact on the business world.

## 574.

DocuSign's commitment to security and privacy is paramount, and the company employs robust measures to protect user data and comply with privacy regulations.

# 575.

DocuSign has integrated with leading business software applications such as Salesforce, Microsoft Office 365, and Google Workspace, allowing seamless document workflows within existing workflows.

# 576.

The company's electronic signature technology has been widely accepted by legal systems worldwide, leading to the widespread adoption of digital signatures as a legally recognized method of document authentication.

# 577.

DocuSign's technology has helped reduce paper waste and promote environmentally friendly business practices.

# 578.

The company actively supports environmental initiatives and sustainability efforts, aiming to minimize its own environmental footprint.

# 579.

DocuSign's success has led to partnerships and collaborations with industry leaders, including technology companies, financial institutions, and legal organizations.

# 580.

The company has a strong commitment to corporate social responsibility and philanthropy, supporting various charitable initiatives and community programs.

# 581.

DocuSign's impact extends beyond businesses, with individuals using the platform to handle personal document signing, such as contracts, agreements, and forms.

# 582.

DocuSign's user-friendly interface and intuitive design have contributed to its widespread adoption, making it accessible to users with varying levels of technical expertise.

# 583.

The company has a strong focus on user experience, continuously refining its platform to provide a seamless and efficient signing process.

# 584.

DocuSign has received recognition as a top employer, prioritizing employee well-being, diversity, and inclusion.

# 585.

The company has been listed multiple times in Forbes' "World's Most Innovative Companies" and Fortune's "100 Best Companies to Work For" rankings.

# 586.

DocuSign's commitment to diversity and inclusion is reflected in its workforce, leadership team, and corporate culture.

# 587.

The company actively supports diversity initiatives and aims to create an inclusive and equitable work environment.

# 588.

DocuSign's customer base spans various industries, including finance, real estate, legal, healthcare, government, and more.

# 589.

The company's platform is continually evolving to meet the evolving needs of its customers, with regular updates and feature enhancements.

## 590.

DocuSign's technology has revolutionized document workflows, enabling businesses to streamline processes, reduce costs, and improve productivity.

## 591.

The company's vision extends beyond electronic signatures, aiming to digitize and automate end-to-end business processes.

## 592.

DocuSign's platform has played a vital role in transforming traditional paper-based industries, accelerating digital transformation efforts across sectors.

## 593.

The company actively contributes to thought leadership and industry discussions around digital transformation, electronic signatures, and the future of work.

## 594.

DocuSign's commitment to data security and privacy has resulted in certifications and compliance with leading industry standards and regulations.

## 595.

The company's customer support and training programs ensure users have the resources and knowledge to maximize the benefits of the platform.

## 596.

DocuSign's presence extends to mobile applications, allowing users to sign documents and manage workflows on smartphones and tablets.

## 597.

The company's growth and success have inspired the emergence of similar electronic signature platforms and competitors in the market.

## 598.

DocuSign actively engages with its user community, soliciting feedback and suggestions for platform improvements and new features.

## 599.

The company's commitment to innovation drives ongoing research and development efforts to enhance its platform and introduce new capabilities.

## 600.

DocuSign's history reflects the transformative power of digital technology in simplifying document processes, improving efficiency, and facilitating global business transactions.

## 601.

The Georgetown-Silver Plume Historic District is located in Clear Creek County, Colorado, United States.

## 602.

The district includes the towns of Georgetown and Silver Plume, which are known for their well-preserved historic buildings and mining heritage.

## 603.

The district was established in 1966 and was listed on the National Register of Historic Places in 1966.

# 604.

Georgetown was founded in 1859 during the Colorado gold rush and quickly became an important mining town.

# 605.

Silver Plume was established in 1864 as a mining camp and later developed into a thriving silver mining town.

# 606.

The district covers approximately 700 acres and contains over 200 historic structures, including residential, commercial, and industrial buildings.

# 607.

The architecture in the district reflects various styles, including Victorian, Gothic Revival, and Italianate.

# 608.

Many of the buildings in the district were constructed using locally quarried granite, giving them a distinct and unique appearance.

# 609.

The Georgetown Loop Railroad, a narrow-gauge historic railroad, runs through the district and offers scenic rides for visitors.

# 610.

The district is known for its charming main streets, lined with colorful storefronts and well-preserved buildings.

# 611.

The Hamill House, a Victorian mansion built in 1867, is one of the district's most notable landmarks and is open to the public as a museum.

## 612.

The Georgetown-Silver Plume Historic District is surrounded by breathtaking mountain scenery, with views of the Rocky Mountains and the Clear Creek Valley.

## 613.

The district served as a crucial transportation hub during the mining boom, with stagecoach lines and railroads connecting it to other parts of Colorado.

## 614.

The Silver Plume Depot, built in 1884, is a historic train station that has been restored and is now home to a museum showcasing the area's mining history.

## 615.

The district played a significant role in Colorado's mining history, with numerous silver and gold mines operating in the area.

## 616.

The Hotel de Paris Museum, located in Georgetown, offers a glimpse into the town's past as a bustling mining center, with exhibits on mining, transportation, and the hotel's history.

## 617.

The Georgetown-Silver Plume Historic District attracts visitors from around the world who come to explore its rich history and experience its preserved heritage.

## 618.

The district's historic buildings have been used as filming locations for various movies and television shows, adding to its charm and appeal.

## 619.

The Georgetown-Silver Plume Historic District hosts several annual events, including historic home tours, festivals, and holiday celebrations.

## 620.

The district is home to several well-preserved Victorian-era churches, including the Grace Episcopal Church and St. John's Catholic Church.

## 621.

Georgetown is known as the "Silver Queen of Colorado" due to its significant silver mining history.

## 622.

The Georgetown Energy Museum showcases the town's role in hydroelectric power generation, which was crucial for mining operations.

## 623.

The Georgetown-Silver Plume Historic District offers opportunities for outdoor recreation, including hiking, fishing, and scenic drives.

## 624.

The district is part of the Georgetown-Silver Plume National Historic Landmark District, recognized for its exceptional historical significance.

## 625.

The Georgetown Loop Historic Mining & Railroad Park provides visitors with a hands-on experience of the area's mining heritage and offers train rides through the scenic mountains.

## 626.

Many of the district's buildings have been lovingly restored and preserved, allowing visitors to step back in time and experience the town's rich history.

## 627.

The Georgetown-Silver Plume Historic District has inspired artists and photographers with its picturesque landscapes and historic architecture.

## 628.

The district's historic buildings and streetscapes have been used as backdrops for numerous period films and television productions.

## 629.

The district is a popular destination for history enthusiasts, offering guided tours, interpretive exhibits, and educational programs.

## 630.

The Georgetown-Silver Plume Historic District has been recognized for its architectural significance and preservation efforts, receiving awards and accolades.

## 631.

The Georgetown-Silver Plume Historic District played a role in the development of Colorado as a state and contributed to the growth of the mining industry in the region.

## 632.

The district is located along the scenic Peak to Peak Highway, a designated Colorado Scenic Byway known for its breathtaking views.

## 633.

The Georgetown-Silver Plume Historic District showcases the resilience and perseverance of the early settlers and miners who helped shape the region.

## 634.

Many of the district's buildings have been repurposed into charming shops, galleries, restaurants, and bed and breakfast establishments.

## 635.

The district's historic cemeteries, such as the Silver Plume Cemetery, provide insight into the lives and stories of the early residents.

## 636.

The Georgetown-Silver Plume Historic District offers opportunities for ghost tours and paranormal investigations, with stories of hauntings and supernatural occurrences.

## 637.

The district is home to several museums and historical societies dedicated to preserving and promoting the area's heritage.

## 638.

Georgetown's Christmas Market, held annually in December, attracts visitors with its festive atmosphere, crafts, food, and holiday entertainment.

## 639.

The Georgetown-Silver Plume Historic District has been recognized as a National Historic Landmark, showcasing its exceptional historical and cultural value.

## 640.

The district's historic Georgetown Loop Railroad is a popular tourist attraction, offering scenic rides through the mountains and showcasing the engineering marvels of the past.

## 641.

The district's historic Georgetown Loop Railroad is a popular tourist attraction, offering scenic rides through the mountains and showcasing the engineering marvels of the past.

## 642.

The district's charming downtown area features quaint shops, antique stores, and art galleries, making it a delightful destination for shopping and exploration.

## 643.

The Georgetown-Silver Plume Historic District has been featured in travel publications and magazines as a must-visit destination for history buffs and lovers of small-town charm.

## 644.

The district's historic structures have been meticulously maintained, with ongoing restoration efforts to preserve their original character.

## 645.

The Georgetown-Silver Plume Historic District provides a sense of nostalgia and transports visitors back in time to the era of the mining boom.

## 646.

The district's historic buildings have witnessed the changing times and reflect the architectural styles and trends of their respective periods.

## 647.

Georgetown and Silver Plume have a vibrant community that celebrates their shared history through events, festivals, and cultural activities.

# 648.

The district's picturesque surroundings make it a popular destination for outdoor enthusiasts, offering opportunities for hiking, wildlife viewing, and photography.

# 649.

The Georgetown-Silver Plume Historic District is a testament to the importance of preserving our cultural heritage and showcasing the stories of the past.

# 650.

The district continues to captivate visitors with its authentic historic ambiance, allowing them to step back in time and experience the fascinating history of Colorado's mining era.

# 651.

The Granada Relocation Center, also known as Camp Amache, was a World War II internment camp located in southeast Colorado, United States.

# 652.

The camp was one of ten internment camps established by the U.S. government to detain Japanese Americans during the war.

# 653.

It was named after the nearby town of Granada, Colorado, and the Amache River that ran through the area.

# 654.

The Granada Relocation Center operated from 1942 to 1945 and housed over 7,000 Japanese Americans from California, primarily from the Los Angeles area.

# 655.

The decision to establish internment camps was made as a result of Executive Order 9066, signed by President Franklin D. Roosevelt in 1942, which authorized the forced relocation of Japanese Americans living on the West Coast.

## 656.

The camp covered an area of approximately 10,000 acres and consisted of 29 blocks, each containing 12 barracks and a mess hall.

## 657.

The Granada Relocation Center was surrounded by barbed wire fences and guarded by military police, restricting the movement of its inhabitants.

## 658.

The camp's living conditions were harsh, with communal latrines, limited privacy, and barracks that lacked insulation, making them extremely hot in summer and cold in winter.

## 659.

Despite the difficult conditions, the Japanese American prisoners in the camp established a sense of community and organized various activities, including sports, arts and crafts, and educational programs.

## 660.

The prisoners also published a newspaper called "Granada Pioneer" to keep the community informed about camp events and provide a sense of normalcy.

## 661.

Many of the Japanese Americans imprisoned in the Granada Relocation Center were American citizens, born and raised in the United States.

## 662.

The prisoners faced discrimination and prejudice both inside and outside the camp, with their loyalty to the United States often questioned.

## 663.

Despite the injustice they faced, many Japanese Americans in the camp remained loyal to the United States and actively contributed to the war effort.

## 664.

Some prisoners in the camp were allowed to work outside the fences as part of the "Leave Clearance Program," helping with agricultural labor and other jobs in the local community.

## 665.

The Granada Relocation Center had its own school system, providing education for children and adults. The schools offered classes in English, math, science, and vocational training.

## 666.

The camp's hospital provided medical care for its residents, with doctors, nurses, and other medical staff working in the facility.

## 667.

The prisoners in the Granada Relocation Center faced significant challenges, including uncertainty about their future, loss of property and businesses, and the emotional toll of being uprooted from their homes.

## 668.

Despite the hardships, the Japanese American prisoners in the camp demonstrated resilience and strength, supporting one another and finding ways to maintain their dignity and cultural heritage.

## 669.

The Granada Relocation Center was officially closed in October 1945, following the end of World War II.

## 670.

After the closure of the camp, many Japanese Americans faced difficulties reintegrating into society and rebuilding their lives.

## 671.

In 1986, the site of the Granada Relocation Center was designated a National Historic Landmark, recognizing its historical significance.

## 672.

Efforts have been made to preserve and interpret the history of the Granada Relocation Center, including the establishment of the Amache Preservation Society and the Amache Museum at the site.

## 673.

The Amache Museum houses exhibits and artifacts that tell the story of the internment camp and its impact on the Japanese American community.

## 674.

The Granada Relocation Center serves as a reminder of the injustices perpetrated against Japanese Americans during World War II and the importance of protecting civil liberties.

## 675.

The Amache site offers visitors the opportunity to learn about the experiences of Japanese Americans in the camp through guided tours and educational programs.

## 676.

The Granada Relocation Center is one of the few remaining physical reminders of the internment camps that were once scattered across the United States.

# 677.

The site of the Granada Relocation Center holds significant historical and cultural value, representing a chapter in American history that should not be forgotten.

# 678.

The Granada Relocation Center and the internment of Japanese Americans have been the subject of numerous books, documentaries, and artistic works that aim to shed light on this dark period.

# 679.

Efforts have been made to gather and preserve the stories and testimonies of those who were imprisoned at the Granada Relocation Center, ensuring their experiences are not lost to history.

# 680.

The Granada Relocation Center stands as a solemn reminder of the importance of upholding civil liberties, respecting human rights, and learning from past mistakes.

# 681.

The internment of Japanese Americans during World War II has since been recognized as a grave injustice, and the United States government has issued formal apologies and reparations to surviving detainees.

# 682.

The Granada Relocation Center and its history continue to resonate with communities and individuals seeking to promote social justice, equality, and understanding.

# 683.

In 2006, the National Park Service established the Japanese American Confinement Sites Grant Program to fund projects that preserve and interpret the history of the internment camps, including the Granada Relocation Center.

## 684.

The Granada Relocation Center represents a pivotal moment in American history, highlighting the importance of protecting civil liberties during times of crisis.

## 685.

The experience of Japanese Americans in the Granada Relocation Center serves as a powerful reminder of the enduring strength and resilience of individuals in the face of adversity.

## 686.

The story of the Granada Relocation Center has inspired discussions and reflections on the broader issues of discrimination, prejudice, and the need for vigilance in safeguarding the rights of all individuals.

## 687.

The Granada Relocation Center is a site of pilgrimage for many Japanese Americans and their descendants, who visit to honor the memory of their ancestors and ensure that their stories are remembered.

## 688.

The Granada Relocation Center and its preservation efforts serve as a cautionary tale, reminding society of the consequences of xenophobia, racism, and the erosion of civil liberties.

## 689.

The Granada Relocation Center has become a place of healing and reconciliation, where descendants of former prisoners and local communities come together to commemorate the past and promote understanding.

## 690.

The Granada Relocation Center and the broader internment experience have influenced the civil rights movement and the ongoing fight for equality and justice for marginalized communities.

## 691.

The story of the Granada Relocation Center has sparked conversations and initiatives aimed at preserving and sharing the stories of other internment camps across the United States.

## 692.

The Granada Relocation Center stands as a testament to the power of remembrance and the importance of confronting and learning from past injustices.

## 693.

The Granada Relocation Center has been recognized as a significant historical site by organizations such as the National Trust for Historic Preservation.

## 694.

Efforts are ongoing to expand the preservation and interpretation of the Granada Relocation Center, ensuring that future generations can learn from its history and the lessons it offers.

## 695.

The Granada Relocation Center has become a site for educational programs, workshops, and discussions that aim to promote dialogue, understanding, and the value of diversity.

## 696.

The Granada Relocation Center has become a touchstone for the Japanese American community, serving as a gathering place for reunions, memorials, and cultural celebrations.

## 697.

The preservation and interpretation of the Granada Relocation Center contribute to a more comprehensive understanding of the complex history of World War II and its impact on different communities.

## 698.

The story ofthe Granada Relocation Center serves as a reminder of the importance of safeguarding civil liberties and ensuring that the mistakes of the past are not repeated.

## 699.

The Granada Relocation Center has inspired artists, writers, and filmmakers to explore and depict the experiences of Japanese Americans during World War II, contributing to a broader cultural understanding of this chapter in history.

## 700.

The Granada Relocation Center stands as a symbol of resilience, courage, and the enduring spirit of the Japanese American community, who have used their experiences to advocate for justice and equality for all.

## 701.

The Galapagos Swallow-tailed Gull (Creagrus furcatus) is a unique species of seabird found exclusively in the Galapagos Islands.

## 702.

It is the only fully nocturnal seabird in the world, meaning it is most active at night.

## 703.

The Swallow-tailed Gull has a distinct appearance with its black plumage, red-ringed eyes, and a long, deeply forked tail.

# 704.

They are medium-sized gulls, typically measuring about 50-56 centimeters in length.

# 705.

The species is sexually dimorphic, with males being slightly larger than females.

# 706.

The Swallow-tailed Gull primarily feeds on small fish, squid, and crustaceans, which it catches by plunge diving into the ocean.

# 707.

Its diet also includes bioluminescent prey, making it well-adapted for nocturnal feeding.

# 708.

During the day, Swallow-tailed Gulls can be found resting on rocky cliffs or volcanic ledges, often in large colonies.

# 709.

They have a limited breeding range, with the Galapagos Islands being their only known nesting site.

# 710.

The breeding season for Swallow-tailed Gulls typically occurs between May and October.

# 711.

Unlike other gulls, Swallow-tailed Gulls do not build nests. Instead, they lay their eggs directly on the rocky ground or ledges.

# 712.

The female Swallow-tailed Gull typically lays a single egg, which both parents take turns incubating for about 30-40 days.

## 713.

Once hatched, the chick is covered in gray down feathers and relies on its parents for food and protection.

## 714.

The parents feed the chick by regurgitating a milky substance known as "pigeon's milk."

## 715.

The chick undergoes a period of growth and development, gradually acquiring its adult plumage.

## 716.

Swallow-tailed Gulls have a unique courtship display where they engage in "billing," a behavior in which they touch each other's bills while making vocalizations.

## 717.

The species is known for its haunting, high-pitched calls, which can be heard during the night on the breeding colonies.

## 718.

Swallow-tailed Gulls are highly adapted to the harsh marine environment of the Galapagos Islands, with specialized salt glands that allow them to excrete excess salt from their bodies.

## 719.

The population size of Swallow-tailed Gulls is estimated to be around 25,000 individuals.

## 720.

They are considered to be near-threatened, primarily due to habitat destruction, disturbance, and the impact of climate change on their prey availability.

## 721.

Swallow-tailed Gulls are endemic to the Galapagos Islands, meaning they are found nowhere else in the world.

## 722.

They have a relatively long lifespan, with individuals known to live for up to 20 years.

## 723.

Swallow-tailed Gulls are agile flyers, capable of soaring gracefully above the ocean and maneuvering through the rocky cliffs of their breeding colonies.

## 724.

They have excellent vision, allowing them to navigate and locate prey even in low-light conditions.

## 725.

The red rings around their eyes are believed to help reduce glare from the moon and aid in their nocturnal foraging.

## 726.

Swallow-tailed Gulls have a symbiotic relationship with the Red-billed Tropicbirds, nesting in close proximity to each other on the same cliffs.

## 727.

Their presence on the Galapagos Islands is significant as they contribute to the overall biodiversity and ecological balance of the archipelago..

## 728.

Swallow-tailed Gulls are protected by the Galapagos National Park, and their conservation status is closely monitored.

## 729.

They are a popular attraction for birdwatchers and nature enthusiasts visiting the Galapagos Islands.

## 730.

Swallow-tailed Gulls are highly adapted to their marine habitat and have unique physiological and behavioral characteristics.

## 731.

The species has undergone evolutionary adaptations to the specific ecological conditions of the Galapagos Islands over thousands of years.

## 732.

Swallow-tailed Gulls have a relatively small population size compared to other seabird species, making them vulnerable to environmental changes and disturbances.

## 733.

The isolation of the Galapagos Islands has played a significant role in shaping the evolutionary history of the Swallow-tailed Gulls.

## 734.

The species is part of the larger ecosystem of the Galapagos Islands, interacting with other wildlife and contributing to the overall biodiversity.

## 735.

Swallow-tailed Gulls are highly specialized for their nocturnal lifestyle, with anatomical and physiological adaptations that enable them to navigate and hunt in darkness.

## 736.

The Galapagos Islands provide an ideal habitat for Swallow-tailed Gulls, with abundant food resources and suitable nesting sites.

## 737.

The species is relatively understudied compared to other seabirds, and ongoing research helps expand our understanding of their behavior, ecology, and conservation needs.

## 738.

Swallow-tailed Gulls exhibit high site fidelity, returning to the same breeding colonies year after year.

## 739.

The Swallow-tailed Gull is classified as a monotypic species, meaning it is the only member of its genus, Creagrus.

## 740.

The conservation of Swallow-tailed Gulls is closely linked to the conservation of the unique ecosystem of the Galapagos Islands.

## 741.

Swallow-tailed Gulls are known for their exceptional flying abilities, with the ability to soar effortlessly on thermal currents and glide over the ocean waves.

## 742.

The diet of Swallow-tailed Gulls is influenced by the availability of prey, which can vary seasonally and in response to oceanographic conditions.

# 743.

The Galapagos Marine Reserve, established to protect the marine ecosystem of the archipelago, indirectly benefits Swallow-tailed Gulls by conserving their prey species.

# 744.

Swallow-tailed Gulls have distinctive wing patterns, with dark upper wings and white underwings, making them easily recognizable in flight.

# 745.

The population dynamics of Swallow-tailed Gulls are influenced by various factors, including food availability, predation, and climatic conditions.

# 746.

The conservation efforts for Swallow-tailed Gulls involve monitoring their breeding success, studying their population trends, and implementing measures to mitigate potential threats.

# 747.

Swallow-tailed Gulls play a role in nutrient cycling within the marine ecosystem, as their droppings contribute to the fertilization of surrounding waters.

# 748.

The nesting colonies of Swallow-tailed Gulls provide important habitat for other bird species, such as boobies and frigatebirds, which may nest in close proximity or utilize abandoned nests.

# 749.

Swallow-tailed Gulls are agile divers, capable of plunging into the water to catch their prey, and they can remain underwater for extended periods.

# 750.

The Galapagos Swallow-tailed Gull is an iconic species of the Galapagos Islands, symbolizing the unique wildlife and ecological significance of this remarkable archipelago.

# 751.

The Galapagos Waved Albatross, also known as the Galapagos Albatross or the Waved Albatross (Phoebastria irrorata), is a large seabird species endemic to the Galapagos Islands.

# 752.

It is one of the largest seabirds in the world, with a wingspan reaching up to 2.5 meters (8 feet).

# 753.

The Waved Albatross is known for its distinctive appearance, with a white body, black wings, and a yellow bill.

# 754.

It is named after the wavy patterns on its wings, which become more prominent as the bird matures.

# 755.

The species is primarily found on Española Island in the Galapagos archipelago, where it breeds and nests.

# 756.

The breeding season for Waved Albatrosses typically occurs between April and December.

# 757.

The Waved Albatross is monogamous, with pairs forming long-term partnerships and returning to the same nesting site each year.

# 758.

The species has a unique courtship display called the "sky-pointing ceremony," where the male and female stand face to face, raise their bills skyward, and clack their bills together.

# 759.

Waved Albatrosses perform elaborate dances and ritualized movements as part of their courtship and bonding process.

# 760.

The Waved Albatross has a slow reproductive cycle, with females laying only one egg every two years.

# 761.

The incubation period for the eggs is approximately two months, during which both parents take turns incubating the egg.

# 762.

Once hatched, the chick is covered in gray down feathers and relies on its parents for food and protection.

# 763.

The parents take turns foraging for food and returning to the nest to feed the chick with a regurgitated oily substance.

# 764.

The Waved Albatross chicks grow rapidly and develop adult feathers, becoming capable of flight after about five months.

# 765.

Waved Albatrosses are exceptional long-distance flyers, capable of covering vast distances over the open ocean in search of food.

# 766.

They have a unique flying style, with slow, deliberate wing beats
and the ability to soar effortlessly on air currents.

## 767.

The Waved Albatrosses feed primarily on squid and fish, which they
catch by plunge diving into the water.

## 768.

The species has a specialized gland above its nasal passages that
helps excrete excess salt, allowing it to drink seawater and obtain
moisture from its prey.

## 769.

Outside of the breeding season, Waved Albatrosses spend much of
their time at sea, often ranging as far as the coast of South America.

## 770.

The Waved Albatross has a strong connection to the marine
environment, spending the majority of its life on the open ocean.

## 771.

The Waved Albatross is considered a vulnerable species, with a
population estimated to be around 35,000 individuals.

## 772.

The species faces threats such as habitat degradation, introduced
predators, and bycatch in fishing nets.

## 773.

Conservation efforts have been implemented to protect the breeding
sites of Waved Albatrosses and reduce human disturbances during
the critical breeding season.

## 774.

The Waved Albatross is a protected species in the Galapagos
National Park, and its conservation status is closely monitored.

## 775.

The species plays a vital ecological role in the Galapagos Islands,
contributing to nutrient cycling and dispersal of marine organisms.

## 776.

The Waved Albatross is considered an indicator species, reflecting
the health of the marine ecosystem and the surrounding waters.

## 777.

The Waved Albatross is a long-lived species, with individuals
known to live for more than 40 years.

## 778.

The Waved Albatross is an iconic symbol of the Galapagos Islands
and an important attraction for eco-tourists and birdwatchers.

## 779.

It is one of the few albatross species found in the tropics, making it a
unique and remarkable seabird.

## 780.

The Waved Albatross has been featured in numerous documentaries
and wildlife programs, showcasing its fascinating behaviors and
natural history.

## 781.

The species is an integral part of the complex ecological web of the
Galapagos Islands, contributing to the overall biodiversity and
ecosystem dynamics.

## 782.

The Galapagos Islands are home to the largest colony of Waved Albatrosses in the world, with Española Island being the main breeding site.

## 783.

Waved Albatrosses have strong site fidelity, returning to the same nesting site year after year, often to the exact same spot.

## 784.

The Waved Albatross population undergoes seasonal fluctuations, with individuals migrating to other areas during the non-breeding season.

## 785.

The species faces threats from introduced species such as rats and cats, which prey on eggs and chicks, and disrupt the nesting colonies.

## 786.

The Galapagos National Park and various conservation organizations are working to control and eradicate invasive species to protect the Waved Albatross and its nesting habitat.

## 787.

The conservation efforts for Waved Albatrosses are closely linked to the overall management and protection of the Galapagos Marine Reserve.

## 788.

Waved Albatrosses have a unique role in the nutrient cycling of the Galapagos marine ecosystem, as their excrement acts as a fertilizer for the islands' vegetation.

## 789.

The Waved Albatross is known for its impressive wing span, with the ability to glide for long distances without flapping its wings.

## 790.

The species has evolved to have strong, webbed feet, which aid in takeoff and landing on both land and water.

## 791.

The Waved Albatross has a strong and sharp beak, allowing it to efficiently catch and consume its prey.

## 792.

The population size of Waved Albatrosses has fluctuated over the years, influenced by factors such as food availability, environmental conditions, and human impacts.

## 793.

The Waved Albatross plays an important ecological role in the Galapagos Islands, contributing to the dispersal of marine nutrients and the maintenance of the marine food web.

## 794.

The Waved Albatross is a flagship species for conservation efforts in the Galapagos Islands, helping to raise awareness and support for the protection of the unique biodiversity of the archipelago.

## 795.

The Waved Albatross is a long-lived bird, reaching sexual maturity around the age of 7 to 11 years.

## 796.

The species has an annual molt, during which time it sheds and replaces its old feathers, ensuring optimal flight performance.

# 797.

Waved Albatrosses are known to engage in "allopreening," a behavior in which individuals groom each other's feathers, strengthening social bonds within the colony.

# 798.

The Waved Albatross has a low reproductive rate, with females typically laying a single egg every other year.

# 799.

The breeding success of Waved Albatrosses is strongly influenced by environmental factors, such as sea surface temperature and food availability.

# 800.

The Waved Albatrosses' presence in the Galapagos Islands highlights the importance of conservation efforts to protect their breeding sites and the unique marine ecosystem they depend on.

# 801.

Boeing, officially known as The Boeing Company, was founded on July 15, 1916, in Seattle, Washington, by William E. Boeing.

# 802.

The company was initially named Pacific Aero Products Company and later changed its name to Boeing Airplane Company in 1917.

# 803.

Boeing's first airplane, the Boeing Model 1, also known as the B&W Seaplane, made its first flight on June 15, 1916.

# 804.

In 1917, Boeing received its first significant military contract from the U.S. Navy for the production of 50 Model C seaplanes.

# 805.

Boeing played a crucial role during World War I, producing military aircraft and seaplanes for the United States and its allies.

# 806.

Boeing's first commercial success came with the introduction of the Boeing Model 40, a mail-carrying biplane that entered service in 1927.

# 807.

The Boeing Model 247, introduced in 1933, was the first modern airliner with an all-metal, stressed-skin design and retractable landing gear.

# 808.

Boeing's most iconic and enduring aircraft, the Boeing 747, made its first flight in 1969. It was the world's first wide-body commercial airliner.

# 809.

The 747, often referred to as the "Jumbo Jet," revolutionized air travel by allowing for more passengers and longer flights.

# 810.

Boeing's next major success came with the development of the Boeing 737, which entered service in 1968 and remains in production today as the 737 MAX..

# 811.

The 737 is one of the best-selling commercial aircraft in history, with over 10,000 units delivered to date.

# 812.

In 1997, Boeing merged with McDonnell Douglas Corporation, forming the world's largest aerospace company at the time.

## 813.

Boeing's headquarters is located in Chicago, Illinois, following its relocation from Seattle in 2001.

## 814.

The company has a significant presence in the defense industry, manufacturing military aircraft, helicopters, and missiles.

## 815.

Boeing has been involved in numerous space programs, including the development of the Saturn V rocket, which carried astronauts to the moon during the Apollo missions.

## 816.

Boeing's contributions to the space industry also include the Space Shuttle program, in which the company built the Orbiter vehicles.

## 817.

The Boeing 787 Dreamliner, introduced in 2011, is a state-of-the-art commercial aircraft known for its fuel efficiency and advanced technologies.

## 818.

The Dreamliner is made predominantly from composite materials, reducing weight and enhancing fuel economy.

## 819.

The 787 Dreamliner was the first commercial aircraft to be certified using a predominantly paperless design and production process.

## 820.

Boeing faced significant challenges with the development of the 787 Dreamliner, including production delays and issues related to the lithium-ion batteries used in the aircraft.

## 821.

The Boeing 777, introduced in 1994, is another highly successful wide-body airliner known for its range and fuel efficiency.

## 822.

Boeing's defense division is responsible for iconic military aircraft such as the B-17 Flying Fortress, B-29 Superfortress, F/A-18 Hornet, and AH-64 Apache.

## 823.

Boeing has a long-standing relationship with the United States Air Force and has produced several aircraft, including the B-52 Stratofortress and the KC-135 Stratotanker.

## 824.

The Boeing 747-8, introduced in 2011, is the latest iteration of the 747 series and offers improved fuel efficiency and increased cargo capacity.

## 825.

In recent years, Boeing has faced significant challenges with the grounding of the 737 MAX following two fatal crashes in 2018 and 2019.

## 826.

The 737 MAX grounding led to extensive investigations, design changes, and the implementation of enhanced safety measures before the aircraft was allowed to return to service.

## 827.

Boeing is a major contributor to the global aerospace industry, employing over 140,000 people worldwide.

## 828.

The company operates manufacturing facilities in multiple countries, including the United States, Australia, Canada, and the United Kingdom.

## 829.

Boeing is involved in various philanthropic initiatives, supporting education, environmental conservation, and community development.

## 830.

Boeing is a significant exporter, with its products and services contributing to the U.S. trade balance.

## 831.

The company has a robust research and development program, focusing on advanced technologies, materials, and manufacturing processes.

## 832.

Boeing has a strong commitment to sustainability and has set ambitious goals to reduce greenhouse gas emissions, conserve water, and minimize waste.

## 833.

Over the years, Boeing has received numerous awards and recognitions for its technological advancements, innovation, and safety.

## 834.

The company has diversified its portfolio beyond aircraft manufacturing, expanding into areas such as satellite systems, aviation services, and autonomous technologies.

## 835.

Boeing has a history of collaborating with other aerospace companies, government agencies, and international partners to develop advanced technologies and address industry challenges.

## 836.

The Boeing Company is publicly traded on the New York Stock Exchange under the ticker symbol "BA."

## 837.

Boeing is a key player in the global aviation industry and has a significant impact on air transportation and economic development.

## 838.

The company operates a comprehensive customer support network, offering maintenance, repair, and overhaul services to airlines and other operators.

## 839.

Boeing has a strong focus on safety and invests heavily in training programs for pilots, maintenance technicians, and other aviation professionals.

## 840.

The company's products and services are used by airlines, militaries, governments, and private individuals around the world.

## 841.

Boeing has a rich legacy of innovation, with many of its technological advancements shaping the aviation industry.

# 842.

The company has been involved in groundbreaking projects such as the X-32 and X-35, competing designs for the Joint Strike Fighter program.

# 843.

Boeing's contributions to the aerospace industry extend beyond commercial and military aircraft. The company has developed satellites, launch vehicles, and spacecraft systems.

# 844.

Boeing has a strong commitment to diversity and inclusion, aiming to create a workplace that reflects the global communities it serves.

# 845.

The company has faced challenges in recent years, including supply chain issues, production delays, and financial setbacks.

# 846.

Boeing has a significant presence in the international market, with customers and partnerships across continents.

# 847.

The company has a rich history of collaboration with educational institutions, research organizations, and industry associations to foster innovation and talent development.

# 848.

Boeing has a strong focus on continuous improvement and invests in research and development to enhance safety, efficiency, and environmental sustainability.

# 849.

The company's global reach and operations contribute to economic growth and job creation in various regions around the world.

## 850.

Boeing's commitment to innovation, safety, and excellence has made it a prominent player in the aerospace industry, shaping the way people travel and the future of aviation.

## 851.

Stripe, officially known as Stripe Inc., was founded in 2010 by Irish brothers John and Patrick Collison.

## 852.

The company's headquarters are located in San Francisco, California.

## 853.

Stripe was initially created to address the challenges faced by online businesses in accepting and processing payments.

## 854.

The Collison brothers developed the idea for Stripe while studying at Harvard University.

## 855.

Stripe's first product, called Stripe Payments, launched in September 2011, offering developers an easy way to integrate payment processing into their websites and applications.

## 856.

The company's founders were only 22 and 19 years old, respectively, when they launched Stripe.

## 857.

Stripe's primary focus is on simplifying the complexities of online transactions, allowing businesses to accept payments seamlessly.

## 858.

The company quickly gained traction and became popular among developers due to its user-friendly APIs and documentation.

## 859.

Stripe's business model revolves around charging a fee for each successful transaction processed through its platform.

## 860.

The company's early investors included venture capital firms such as Sequoia Capital and Andreessen Horowitz.

## 861.

In 2014, Stripe introduced a suite of additional products and services, including Stripe Connect, which allows businesses to build online marketplaces.

## 862.

Stripe expanded its reach globally, gradually expanding its services to countries outside of the United States.

## 863.

Stripe has become known for its focus on developer-friendly tools and resources, allowing businesses to integrate payment systems with ease.

## 864.

The company emphasizes a user-centric approach, providing excellent customer support and technical assistance to its users.

## 865.

Stripe has attracted a wide range of customers, including small businesses, startups, and large enterprises.

## 866.

The company's platform supports various payment methods, including credit cards, digital wallets, and local payment methods specific to different countries.

## 867.

Stripe's technology enables businesses to accept payments in multiple currencies, making it convenient for global transactions.

## 868.

The company offers advanced fraud prevention and security features to protect businesses and customers from fraudulent activities.

## 869.

Stripe has consistently focused on expanding its product offerings and improving its infrastructure to meet the evolving needs of businesses.

## 870.

In 2016, Stripe launched Stripe Atlas, a service designed to help entrepreneurs from around the world incorporate their businesses in the United States.

## 871.

Stripe has played a significant role in the growth of the e-commerce industry, enabling businesses to easily establish online payment systems.

## 872.

The company has fostered a strong developer community, regularly organizing events and conferences to connect with and support developers.

## 873.

Stripe has acquired several companies to enhance its offerings and expand its reach, including Kickoff, Index, and Payable.

## 874.

The company's success has attracted partnerships with major technology companies, such as Apple, Google, and Shopify.

## 875.

Stripe has received numerous awards and accolades for its innovation, including being named to the Forbes Cloud 100 list multiple times.

## 876.

The company's valuation has steadily increased over the years, making it one of the most valuable startups in the world.

## 877.

Stripe's platform has processed billions of dollars in transactions, contributing to the growth of digital commerce globally.

## 878.

The company has been instrumental in supporting the growth of the subscription-based business model, providing businesses with the tools to manage recurring payments.

## 879.

Stripe has expanded its services beyond payment processing, offering additional tools and services such as Stripe Radar for fraud detection and prevention.

## 880.

The company has made efforts to provide inclusive financial services, supporting businesses in emerging markets and underserved communities.

# 881.

Stripe actively supports and promotes open-source software, recognizing its importance in fostering innovation and collaboration.

# 882.

The company has a strong commitment to transparency and publishes regular reports on the state of payments and trends in the industry.

# 883.

Stripe's success has led to partnerships with financial institutions, allowing for seamless integration of banking services with its platform.

# 884.

Stripe has been recognized for its workplace culture and commitment to employee well-being, with initiatives such as flexible work arrangements and generous parental leave policies.

# 885.

The company has expanded its presence globally, establishing offices in cities such as Dublin, London, Singapore, and Tokyo.

# 886.

Stripe actively supports entrepreneurship and has launched programs and initiatives to empower and educate aspiring entrepreneurs.

# 887.

The company has a strong focus on data privacy and security, adhering to industry standards and regulations to protect customer information.

## 888.

Stripe has played a significant role in promoting the growth of the digital economy, enabling businesses of all sizes to participate in online commerce.

## 889.

The company's founders, John and Patrick Collison, have been recognized as influential figures in the technology and business world, receiving numerous awards and accolades.

## 890.

Stripe has actively contributed to the development of the financial technology industry, driving innovation and pushing boundaries in online payments.

## 891.

The company has been involved in philanthropic initiatives, supporting various causes and organizations related to education, technology, and social impact.

## 892.

Stripe has a strong focus on sustainability and has committed to becoming carbon neutral, investing in renewable energy projects and carbon offsets.

## 893.

The company actively engages with regulators and industry bodies to shape policies and standards related to digital payments.

## 894.

Stripe has a robust ecosystem of partners and integrations, allowing businesses to seamlessly connect their operations with other software platforms.

# 895.

The company has a strong emphasis on continuous improvement, regularly releasing updates and new features to enhance its platform.

# 896.

Stripe has been recognized for its commitment to diversity and inclusion, promoting gender equality and underrepresented groups in technology.

# 897.

The company has made efforts to provide resources and support for businesses impacted by the COVID-19 pandemic, including waiving certain fees and offering financial assistance programs.

# 898.

Stripe has a forward-thinking approach, actively exploring emerging technologies such as blockchain and artificial intelligence to enhance its offerings.

# 899.

The company's success has inspired a new generation of entrepreneurs, encouraging innovation and entrepreneurship in the digital economy.

# 900.

Stripe's history is a testament to the power of technological innovation and its ability to transform industries, making online payments accessible and seamless for businesses worldwide.

# 901.

The Leadville Historic District is located in Leadville, Colorado, and covers approximately 67 blocks.

# 902.

Leadville was founded in 1877 after silver was discovered in the area, leading to a major silver rush.

## 903.

The district showcases the unique architecture and history of the late 19th and early 20th centuries.

## 904.

Leadville became one of the largest and wealthiest mining towns in the United States during the silver boom.

## 905.

The district includes over 70 historically significant buildings, including Victorian-era residences, commercial buildings, and churches.

## 906.

Many of the buildings in the district are constructed with locally quarried granite, giving the area a distinctive appearance.

## 907.

The Tabor Opera House, built in 1879, is one of the notable landmarks within the Leadville Historic District. It hosted famous performers of the time, including Oscar Wilde and Harry Houdini.

## 908.

The district is home to the Delaware Hotel, which was constructed in 1886 and is still in operation today.

## 909.

The Matchless Mine, once owned by Horace Tabor, is located within the district. It was one of the richest silver mines in Colorado.

## 910.

The district was added to the National Register of Historic Places in 1968.

# 911.

The Leadville Historic District reflects the prosperity and grandeur of the silver mining era.

# 912.

The district has preserved the original street layout and grid pattern from the late 19th century.

# 913.

Leadville was once home to more than 30,000 residents during its peak mining years.

# 914.

The Historic District offers walking tours and guided tours that provide visitors with insights into the town's rich history.

# 915.

Leadville's elevation of 10,152 feet (3,094 meters) makes it the highest incorporated city in the United States.

# 916.

The Historic District features a variety of architectural styles, including Victorian, Italianate, and Queen Anne.

# 917.

Leadville experienced a significant decline after the silver crash of 1893, but the preservation of its historic buildings has helped revitalize the town as a tourist destination.

# 918.

The district encompasses several museums, including the National Mining Hall of Fame and Museum, which showcases the town's mining heritage.

## 919.

The Healy House Museum and Dexter Cabin are two prominent attractions within the district, offering a glimpse into the lives of Leadville's early settlers.

## 920.

The District boasts beautiful landscapes, surrounded by the Rocky Mountains and offering stunning views of the nearby peaks.

## 921.

The area has attracted filmmakers, and several movies, including "Silver City" and parts of "True Grit," have been filmed in Leadville.

## 922.

Leadville has a rich sporting history and was the birthplace of the Leadville Trail 100, an iconic ultramarathon that attracts runners from around the world.

## 923.

The Historic District hosts numerous events throughout the year, including the Leadville Boom Days, a festival that celebrates the town's mining history.

## 924.

The district is a designated Colorado Creative District, recognizing its vibrant arts and cultural scene.

## 925.

Leadville has produced notable residents, including Horace Tabor, who became a prominent figure during the silver boom, and Molly Brown, known for her survival of the sinking of the Titanic.

# 926.

The town's mining history and historic district have inspired writers, including Edward Abbey, who featured Leadville in his novel "Fire on the Mountain."

# 927.

The district offers opportunities for outdoor recreation, including hiking, biking, and fishing in the nearby lakes and rivers.

# 928.

Leadville has a strong connection to the Wild West era, and visitors can explore the town's history through museums, historic sites, and reenactments.

# 929.

The district is a popular destination for ghost tours, with numerous stories and legends of paranormal activity in the historic buildings.

# 930.

Leadville's historic district has been featured in several documentaries and television shows, showcasing its rich history and architectural beauty.

# 931.

The district is a gateway to outdoor adventure, with nearby access to skiing, snowboarding, and snowshoeing in the winter, and hiking and camping in the summer.

# 932.

Leadville's Historic District is an important reminder of Colorado's mining heritage and the significant role it played in the state's development.

## 933.

The district's preservation efforts have received recognition and awards for their commitment to maintaining the town's historic character.

## 934.

Leadville's Historic District offers a charming atmosphere with its well-preserved buildings, wide streets, and small-town charm.

## 935.

The district is home to various shops, galleries, and restaurants that showcase local artisans and cuisine.

## 936.

Leadville's rich history has inspired the creation of several historical fiction novels and stories set in the town.

## 937.

The district provides a glimpse into the challenges and triumphs of the early settlers who sought their fortunes in the silver mines.

## 938.

Leadville's historic buildings have withstood the test of time, showcasing the craftsmanship and architectural styles of the late 19th century.

## 939.

The district's architecture and streetscapes have been used as inspiration for artists and photographers.

## 940.

The area is a popular destination for history enthusiasts, architecture buffs, and those interested in the Wild West era.

# 941.

The district has been recognized as a Colorado State Historic
District, highlighting its importance in preserving the state's history.

# 942.

Leadville's Historic District is a designated stop on the Colorado
Scenic and Historic Byway, offering breathtaking views and a sense
of nostalgia.

# 943.

The district's rich history has been documented through photographs,
artifacts, and oral histories, preserving the town's heritage for future
generations.

# 944.

Leadville's Historic District has served as a backdrop for various
period films and television series due to its authentic architecture and
historic ambiance.

# 945.

The town takes pride in its heritage and hosts annual events and
festivals that celebrate its history, culture, and community spirit.

# 946.

Leadville's Historic District is known for its friendly and welcoming
community, where residents are proud to share the town's history
with visitors.

# 947.

The district's buildings have been carefully restored and maintained,
preserving the architectural details and charm of the past.

# 948.

Leadville's Historic District offers a step back in time, allowing visitors to imagine life in a bustling mining town during the late 19th century.

## 949.

The district's walking tours and self-guided routes provide an immersive experience, offering insights into the stories and characters that shaped Leadville's history.

## 950.

Leadville's Historic District serves as a reminder of the enduring spirit and resilience of the town's early settlers, leaving a lasting legacy for generations to come.

## 951.

The Lindenmeier site is an archaeological site located in northern Colorado, near the town of Fort Collins.

## 952.

The site is part of the larger complex known as the Folsom culture, which dates back to the Paleoindian period, approximately 10,000 to 11,000 years ago.

## 953.

Lindenmeier is considered one of the most significant archaeological sites in North America and has provided valuable insights into the prehistoric inhabitants of the region.

## 954.

The site was first discovered in 1924 by amateur archaeologist George C. Barber.

## 955.

Lindenmeier encompasses an area of about 11 acres and contains numerous prehistoric features, including hearths, storage pits, and stone tools.

## 956.

Excavations at Lindenmeier have revealed over 70 individual campsites, suggesting that the site was occupied by small groups of hunter-gatherers over an extended period.

## 957.

The site is renowned for its extensive collection of Folsom projectile points, which are distinctive stone tools used for hunting large game, such as mammoths and bison.

## 958.

Lindenmeier is the largest known Folsom site, with over 10,000 artifacts discovered during excavations.

## 959.

The site has yielded numerous bone fragments from extinct animals, providing important evidence of the types of fauna that existed during the Folsom period.

## 960.

Excavations at Lindenmeier have revealed evidence of early human occupation, including fire-cracked rocks, stone tools, and animal bone remains.

## 961.

The discovery of Folsom points at Lindenmeier in the 1930s provided crucial evidence for the existence of a pre-Clovis culture in North America.

## 962.

Lindenmeier's location near the confluence of the Cache la Poudre
River and the South Platte River made it an ideal site for prehistoric
hunting and gathering activities.

## 963.

The archaeological findings at Lindenmeier have helped reshape our
understanding of the Paleoindian period and the early peopling of
North America.

## 964.

The site's excavation and analysis have contributed significantly to
the study of ancient human migration and settlement patterns.

## 965.

Lindenmeier is recognized as a National Historic Landmark and is
listed on the National Register of Historic Places.

## 966.

The site is managed by the U.S. Forest Service and is open to the
public for visitation.

## 967.

Visitors to Lindenmeier can explore interpretive trails that guide
them through the archaeological remains and provide information
about the site's significance.

## 968.

The artifacts recovered from Lindenmeier are curated and displayed
at the nearby Fort Collins Museum of Discovery.

## 969.

The Lindenmeier site is named after Emma and Carl Lindenmeier,
who generously donated the land to the federal government to ensure
its preservation.

# 970.

Lindenmeier represents a unique window into the lives of ancient Paleoindian cultures and their interactions with the environment.

# 971.

The Folsom culture, to which the Lindenmeier site belongs, is characterized by its advanced stone tool technology, including the distinctive Folsom projectile points.

# 972.

The Folsom culture is named after the Folsom site in New Mexico, where the first Folsom points were discovered in the early 20th century.

# 973.

The presence of Folsom points at Lindenmeier provides evidence of long-distance trade and cultural connections between different Paleoindian groups.

# 974.

Lindenmeier has been studied by numerous archaeologists, including renowned researchers such as Frank H. Roberts Jr. and C. Vance Haynes Jr.

# 975.

The excavation of the site was a collaborative effort between professional archaeologists and local volunteers, reflecting the community's interest in preserving their prehistoric heritage.

# 976.

The cultural significance of Lindenmeier extends beyond its archaeological value. It is considered a sacred site by Native American tribes with ancestral ties to the area.

## 977.

The preservation and ongoing research at Lindenmeier have contributed to the protection of cultural resources and the recognition of Native American perspectives in archaeological investigations.

## 978.

Lindenmeier's archaeological record has shed light on the adaptation strategies and subsistence practices of early inhabitants, revealing their deep knowledge of local flora and fauna.

## 979.

The site's excavations have uncovered evidence of bison hunting, including bison bone beds and stone tools used for processing and butchering.

## 980.

Lindenmeier's proximity to natural resources, such as freshwater streams and abundant game, would have provided the ancient inhabitants with a reliable food source.

## 981.

The Folsom culture is known for its highly efficient hunting techniques, utilizing large, specialized spear points for bringing down large mammals.

## 982.

The discovery of stone tools and debris from tool production suggests that Lindenmeier may have served as a workshop for manufacturing and repairing tools.

## 983.

The preservation of organic materials at Lindenmeier has allowed for the study of ancient plant remains, including seeds, pollen, and wood fragments, providing insights into past environments and plant usage.

## 984.

The archaeological evidence at Lindenmeier indicates seasonal occupation, with groups returning to the site during specific times of the year to take advantage of favorable hunting and gathering conditions.

## 985.

The excavation of Lindenmeier has involved meticulous recording and mapping of archaeological features and stratigraphy, enabling researchers to reconstruct past human activities and site organization.

## 986.

The scientific study of Lindenmeier has involved multidisciplinary approaches, including archaeology, anthropology, geology, and paleoecology.

## 987.

The ongoing analysis of artifacts and ecofacts from Lindenmeier continues to yield new information about prehistoric lifeways, subsistence practices, and social organization.

## 988.

The preservation of the Lindenmeier site serves as a reminder of the importance of protecting and studying our cultural heritage to better understand the complexities of human history.

## 989.

The research conducted at Lindenmeier has influenced archaeological methods and theories, contributing to the broader field of Paleoindian studies.

# 990.

The Folsom culture, represented at Lindenmeier, is considered one of the earliest and most technologically advanced cultures in North America.

# 991.

The study of Folsom culture and its artifacts has helped refine our understanding of lithic technology, mobility patterns, and cultural exchange among ancient Native American groups.

# 992.

The excavation and interpretation of Lindenmeier have fostered collaborations between archaeologists, Native American communities, and the general public, promoting shared knowledge and cultural understanding.

# 993.

Lindenmeier's archaeological record offers a glimpse into the daily lives, spiritual beliefs, and artistic expressions of the people who inhabited the area thousands of years ago.

# 994.

The preservation of the Lindenmeier site is an ongoing effort, requiring ongoing monitoring, conservation, and public education to ensure its long-term protection.

# 995.

Lindenmeier represents a testament to human resilience and adaptability, showcasing the ability of early populations to thrive in diverse environments.

# 996.

The Folsom culture's reliance on hunting large game reflects their deep understanding of animal behavior and their ability to successfully exploit local resources.

# 997.

The discoveries at Lindenmeier have challenged previous assumptions about the timing and nature of human occupation in North America, leading to revisions in archaeological interpretations.

# 998.

Lindenmeier's archaeological research has contributed to our understanding of ancient trade networks, resource procurement strategies, and cultural interactions during the Paleoindian period.

# 999.

The artifacts recovered from Lindenmeier, including projectile points, scrapers, and stone flakes, have been instrumental in refining our knowledge of Folsom culture and its technological advancements.

# 1000.

The ongoing study of Lindenmeier continues to provide new insights into the complex history of early human populations in North America, offering a deeper understanding of their lifestyles, cultural practices, and contributions to our shared human heritage.